The
Marketplace
of Ideas

ALSO BY LOUIS MENAND

American Studies

The Metaphysical Club

Pragmatism: A Reader (editor)

The Future of Academic Freedom (editor)

*Discovering Modernism:
T. S. Eliot and His Context*

Issues of Our Time

Ours has been called an information age, but, though information has never been more plentiful, ideas are what shape and reshape our world. "Issues of Our Time" is a series of books in which some of today's leading thinkers explore ideas that matter in the new millennium. The authors—including the philosopher Kwame Anthony Appiah, the sociologist William Julius Wilson, the social psychologist Claude Steele, legal scholars Alan Dershowitz and Charles Fried, and the Nobel Prize–winning economist Amartya Sen—honor clarity without shying away from complexity; these books are both genuinely engaged and genuinely engaging. Each recognizes the importance not just of our values but also of the way we resolve the conflicts among those values. Law, justice, identity, morality, and freedom: concepts such as these are at once abstract and utterly close to home. Our understanding of them helps define who we are and who we hope to be; we are made by what we make of them. These are books, accordingly, that invite the reader to reexamine hand-me-down assumptions and to grapple with powerful trends. Whether you are moved to reason together with these authors, or to argue with them, they are sure to leave your views tested, if not changed. The perspectives of the authors in this series are diverse, the voices are distinctive, the issues are vital.

Henry Louis Gates Jr., series editor

W. E. B. DU BOIS PROFESSOR OF THE HUMANITIES

HARVARD UNIVERSITY

ISSUES OF OUR TIME

LOUIS MENAND

THE MARKETPLACE OF IDEAS

W. W. NORTON & COMPANY

New York · London

For information about permission to reproduce selections from this book,
write to Permissions, W. W. Norton & Company, Inc.,
500 Fifth Avenue, New York, NY 10110

For information about special discounts for bulk purchases, please contact
W. W. Norton Special Sales at specialsales@wwnorton.com or 800-233-4830

Manufacturing by Courier Westford
Book design by Charlotte Staub
Production manager: Julia Druskin

Library of Congress Cataloging-in-Publication Data

Menand, Louis.
The marketplace of ideas / Louis Menand. — 1st ed.
p. cm. — (Issues of our time)
Includes bibliographical references and index.
ISBN 978-0-393-06275-5 (hardcover)
1. Education, Higher—Philosophy. 2. Interdisciplinary approach in
education. 3. Education, Humanistic—Philosophy. 4. College
teachers—Training of. 5. College teachers—Attitudes. I. Title.
LB2322.2.M45 2010
378.01—dc22
                                                    2009030027

W. W. Norton & Company, Inc.
500 Fifth Avenue, New York, N.Y. 10110
www.wwnorton.com

W. W. Norton & Company Ltd.
Castle House, 75/76 Wells Street, London W1T 3QT

1 2 3 4 5 6 7 8 9 0

TO THE TASK FORCE

ALISON

DAVID

DAVID

MARY

STEPHANIE

STEVE

CONTENTS

The
Marketplace
of Ideas

INTRODUCTION

KNOWLEDGE is our most important business. The success of almost all our other business depends on it, but its value is not only economic. The pursuit, production, dissemination, application, and preservation of knowledge are the central activities of a civilization. Knowledge is social memory, a connection to the past; and it is social hope, an investment in the future. The ability to create knowledge and put it to use is *the* adaptive characteristic of humans. It is how we reproduce ourselves as social beings and how we change—how we keep our feet on the ground and our heads in the clouds.

Knowledge is a form of capital that is always unevenly distributed, and people who have more knowledge, or greater access to knowledge, enjoy advantages over people who have less. This means that knowledge stands in an intimate relation to power. We speak of "knowledge for its own sake," but there is nothing we learn that does not put us into a different relation with the world—usually, we hope, a better relation. As a society, Americans are committed to the principle that the production of knowledge should be uninhibited and access to it should be universal. This is a democratic ideal. We think that where knowledge is concerned, more is always better. We don't believe that there are things that we would rather not know, or things that only some of us should know—just as we don't believe that there are points of view that should not be expressed, or citizens who are too wrongheaded to vote. We believe that the more information and ideas we produce, and the more people we make them available to, the better our chances of making good decisions.

Americans therefore make a large social investment in institutions whose purpose is simply the production and dissemination of knowledge—that is, research and teaching. We grant these institutions all kinds of exemptions and protections, and we become worried, sometimes angry, when we suspect that they are not working the way we want them to. Some of our expectations about colleges and universities are unrealistic (and so are some of our expectations about democracy). Teaching is a messy process, an area in which success can be hard to measure or even to define. Research is dicey, too. The price for every good idea or scientific claim is a lot of not-so-good ones. There are more than 4,000 institutions of higher learning in the United States, more than 18 million students, and more than 1 million faculty members.[1] We can't reasonably expect that all of those students will be well educated, or that every piece of scholarship or research will be

---

[1] Most of the data on American higher education in this book are from the *Digest of Education Statistics* of the National Center for Education Statistics, U.S. Department of Education (http://nces.ed.gov/); *U.S. Statistical Abstracts* of the U.S. Census Bureau (http://www.census.gov/compendia/statab/); and the Carnegie Foundation for the Advancement of Teaching (http://www.carnegiefoundation.org/). In my citations, I give the source of my data, but I generally do not provide specific urls, since these change as databases are updated.

worthwhile. But we want to believe that the system, as large, as multitasking, and as heterogeneous as it is, is working for us and not against us, that it is enabling us to do the kind of research and teaching that we want to do—that it is not, in itself, an enemy of reform.

There is always a tension between the state of knowledge and the system in which learning and teaching actually take place. The state of knowledge changes much more readily than the system. Institutions are recalcitrant, and the professional conservatism of professors is an ancient source of ridicule. In 1908, the Cambridge classicist F. M. Cornford, in his satirical guide for young academics, *Microcosmographia Academica*, advised that the basic rule of faculty governance is, "Nothing should ever be done for the first time."[2] In 1963, Clark Kerr, who, as chancellor of the University of California, would soon come to know more than he bargained for about politics and the academy, complained that "few institutions are so conservative as the universities about their own affairs while their members are so liberal about the affairs of others. . . . The faculty member who gets arrested as a 'freedom rider' in the South is a flaming supporter of unanimous prior faculty consent to any change whatsoever on his campus in the North. The door to the faculty club leads both in and out."[3]

---

[2] F. M. Cornford, *Microcosmographia Academica: Being a Guide for the Young Academic Politician*, 4th ed. (1908; Cambridge: Bowes & Bowes, 1949), p. 15. See Gordon Johnson, *University Politics: F. M. Cornford's Cambridge and His Advice to the Young Academic Politician* (Cambridge: Cambridge University Press, 1994).

[3] Clark Kerr, *The Uses of the University* (Cambridge, MA: Harvard University Press, 1963), p. 99. Kerr published four more, expanded editions of this book, the last in 2001. He died in 2003.

To people outside the faculty club, the resistance of professors to institutional reform can appear silly or petty. It can appear worse than that to academic administrators, and university presidents have famously broken their heads trying to get faculty to drink the water to which they have been led. Some of the reasons for this resistance are discussed later in the book; they have to do with the belief, central to the academic's professional self-conception, that the university does not operate like a marketplace. But there is also a practical reason for resistance to reform, which is that any change potentially has a cost. If you require every student to take a certain course, then there is one less elective they will take. If you add a new field of study, then you have to take money from something else to pay for it. When the financial universe was expanding, universities could often add on new things without taking away from old ones, but the universe, as higher education (and everyone else) learned in 2008, can also shrink.

This book is an attempt to answer four questions about American higher education today. Why is it so hard to institute a general education curriculum? Why did the humanities disciplines undergo a crisis of legitimation? Why has "interdisciplinarity" become a magic word? And why do professors all tend to have the same politics? These questions involve ideas; they are essentially intellectual matters that should be amenable to debate and negotiation. They are not, in any significant way, about money. But they are oddly non-transparent, issues that are weirdly and sometimes unpleasantly difficult to discuss or reach agreement about.

My argument is that these issues are all fundamentally systemic—they arise from the way in which institutions

of higher education sustain and reproduce themselves—
and the most significant fact about American higher education as a system is that it is one hundred years old. The
American university is a product of the nineteenth century,
and it has changed very little structurally since the time of
the First World War. It has changed in many other ways—
demographically, intellectually, financially, technologically,
and in terms of its missions, its stakeholders, and its scale—
and these changes have affected the substance of teaching
and research. But the system is still a late nineteenth-century
system, put into place for late nineteenth-century reasons.
The extraordinary series of transformations of higher education after 1945 have strained it. To the extent that this
system still determines the possibilities for producing and
disseminating knowledge, trying to reform the contemporary university is like trying to get on the Internet with a
typewriter, or like riding a horse to the mall.

One thing about systems, especially systems as old as
American higher education, is that people grow unconscious
of them. The system gets internalized. It becomes a mind-set.
It is just "the way things are," and it can be hard to recover
the reasons *why* it is the way things are. When academic
problems appear intractable, it is often because an underlying systemic element is responsible, but no one quite sees
what or where. People who work in the academy, like people
in any institution or profession, are socialized to operate in
certain ways, and when they are called upon to alter their
practices, they sometimes find that they lack a compass to
guide them. Some of the reasons why "this is the way things
are" in American higher education are still good ones; some
are almost certainly obsolete. There are things that academics

should probably not be afraid to do differently—their world will not come to an end—but there are also things that are worth preserving, even at a cost, because the system cannot operate without them. To know which things are which, it helps to have some knowledge of how we got here. Knowledge, after all, is what it's all about.

Like most people who write about American higher education, I focus on what is in reality a very thin slice of the whole—undergraduate and graduate education in the liberal arts and sciences.[4] Most of the 4,000 institutions of higher education in the United States are not liberal arts schools: that is, they award fewer than half their degrees in liberal arts fields. Twenty-two percent of college graduates major in business; only 2 percent major in history. Most of what I have to say concerns higher education as it is experienced by the history major, rather than the business major, and most of my examples are taken from elite liberal arts institutions. This is because, historically, the elites have had the resources to innovate and the visibility to set standards for the system as a whole, but there are many institutions for which the problems I discuss are either irrelevant or non-problems. I am a humanist by training and by interest, and some of the issues I write about are more urgent for faculty and students in the humanities than they are for people in other areas. The natural sciences, in particular, are an exception to many of the trends I discuss (though their exceptionalism is also part of the reason for some of those trends).

---

[4] As do most writers on higher education, I often use the phrase "liberal arts" as shorthand for "liberal arts and sciences," which are defined as subjects of disinterested inquiry rather than areas of professional or vocational education.

There are some interesting academic problems today that do not (I think) test the limits of the system. A pressing pedagogical challenge right now is the problem of adapting a linear model for transmitting knowledge—the lecture monologue, in which a single line of thought leads to an intellectual climax after fifty minutes—to a generation of students who are accustomed to dealing with multiple information streams in short bursts. Once, being a professor meant (among other things) possessing, by dint of years immersed in library mineshafts, refinements on knowledge that were effectively inaccessible to the unlearned person. Now, most of that esoterica is available instantly on Wikipedia. Sheer information is no longer a major piece of the value-added of higher education.[5] This seems a challenge that the system can meet. The most important intellectual development in the academy in the twenty-first century has to do with the relationship between the life sciences—particularly neurobiology, genetics, and psychology—to fields outside the natural sciences, such as philosophy, economics, and literary studies. So far, contention and collaboration in this area seem robust. The system is doing what it was designed to do. It is helping people think better by helping them think together.

In the case of the four problems I address, though, the system seems not to be so accommodating. For most of the book, I write as a historian. I have not struggled to keep my opinions to myself, but I am not a prescriptivist. My emphasis is on the backstory of present problems. At the end of each

[5] See the lively account in Elizabeth Renker, *The Origins of American Literature Studies: An Institutional History* (Cambridge: Cambridge University Press, 2007), pp. 126–43. Renker seems to think that my own view of what she calls "the end of the curriculum" is elegiac; this is a misunderstanding.

chapter, I speculate about what higher education might be like if academics thought of their business differently, since one of the lessons of historical inquiry is that there is no one way that things must be. I do not have an agenda, though. I am in favor of reform when it shakes the system and not when it breaks the system. I do think that intellectual life should involve taking chances.

I became interested in the history of higher education in part because I'm an English professor, and getting interested in the history of higher education, or at least the history of English departments, is something that happened to a lot of English professors after the 1980s. I am interested also because my career has had a slightly askew relation to academic life. This doesn't give me any special insight into the academic world, but it has made me curious about the reasons most academics do what they do in the way they do it. Finally, I worked on the intellectual history of the nineteenth century for a long time, and anyone who does that is bound to get interested in the history of higher education, because the rise of the modern research university is a big part of that picture. The modern American higher education system was and remains a great social accomplishment. It can handle a few questions.

1

The Problem of
General Education

1.

GENERAL EDUCATION courses are courses that all students are required to take no matter what they major in and no matter what their other interests are. The courses are called "general" because they are pitched to non-specialists: they are supposed to be courses that any student can enroll in with hopes of learning something and getting a decent grade. A college's general education curriculum, what the faculty chooses to require of everyone, is a reflection of its overall educational philosophy, even when the faculty chooses to require nothing. Given the possibility of something, nothing is meaningful. Changing an old general education program or instituting a new one is a labor-intensive enterprise, because general education goes to the heart of what a faculty thinks college is all about. So engaging in the process of general education reform says a lot about a faculty, an institution, and the state of knowledge. Many hopes and ideals, along with many preconceptions and insecurities, come to the surface. General education has many stakeholders.

The process of designing a new general education curriculum and selling it to the faculty has been compared to a play by Samuel Beckett, but the comparison is inapt. Beckett's plays are short. It is better compared to *Jarndyce v. Jarndyce*, the lawsuit in Charles Dickens's *Bleak House*, or to being in psychoanalysis: interminable, repetitive, and inconclusive.[1] There is a political issue that needs to be addressed, which is that everyone on the faculty wants a piece of the general education curriculum even though most of the faculty will not teach in it. Every department has more immediate concerns than mounting and staffing courses for students majoring in other subjects; their first priorities are their own majors and (if they have them) their graduate students. On the other hand, every department wants its subject matter to be represented in any set of requirements. Members of department X will generally sign off on a new program of requirements only as long as a course in X is among the courses that every student is required to take.

There is also the issue of the philosophy behind the program, the rationale for the particular requirements being proposed. This is a big bone for a faculty to gnaw on, and it is the kind of subject on which all parties find that they hold surprisingly

---

[1] Harvard began a reform of its general education curriculum in 2003. The faculty approved a new system in 2007; it was not launched until the fall of 2009. The amount of time between the decision to develop a new program and its implementation is not unusual, and it is also not unusual for proposed reforms to fail. The sociologist Daniel Bell devised an ambitious general education curriculum at Columbia in the sixties; a committee chaired by the political scientist Robert Dahl proposed one at Yale in the seventies. Neither program was adopted: see Daniel Bell, *Reforming General Education: The Columbia College Experience in Its National Setting* (Garden City, NY: Anchor Books, 1968), and *The Great Core Curriculum Debate: Education as a Mirror of Culture* (New Rochelle, NY: Change Magazine Press, 1979), pp. 79–102. I was one of many professors involved in the design of the new general education curriculum at Harvard. We compared the process to the Big Dig (a local reference).

firm views, whether they have ever given it much thought before or not. Half-buried assumptions about the purpose of higher education held by professors—and students, parents, alumni, and other members of the university community—tend to emerge into the light when general education is discussed. Academics are not often called upon to articulate a philosophy of higher education, so whatever differences they may have about the ultimate purpose of what they do when they teach undergraduates are rarely on the table.

But the fundamental problem with general education is not the politics of deciding which subjects should be in the curriculum, and it is not the philosophical debates about the meaning of college. The problem with general education is that it is perceived as an attempt to impose on liberal education a mission—call it "preparation for life"—whose rationale liberal education has traditionally defined itself in opposition to. This is why it provokes such paradoxical reactions—why liberal arts faculties want to own general education and to have little to do with it at the same time. That ambivalence has a history.

2.

There are two basic systems of general education: the distribution model and the core model.[2] The distribution model

---

[2] Expository writing and a foreign language are often required of all college students. (It was once common to require students to pass a swimming test before they could graduate—Columbia still does—and some colleges have a physical education requirement.) The usual practice is to require all, or most, freshmen to take a writing or writing-intensive course, but to allow students to place out of the language requirement by scoring a certain mark on a test, such

is the default system, the one that most colleges use. Ordinarily, it requires students to take three departmental courses in each of the three liberal arts divisions—natural science, social science, and the arts and humanities—in order to graduate. This is the system in place at Swarthmore and Yale, for example.[3] Having a distribution requirement is a completely honorable way to duck the entire problem. Its rationale is "breadth and depth": students study one subject intensively, their major, and they complement this study by sampling the subject matter of other disciplines.

But the breadth part (putting aside the question of whether breadth per se is a meaningfully educational goal) is somewhat wishful. Without added constraints, students can cherry-pick their way through a distribution system. They can take only introductory courses or courses known for ease of passage— Physics for Poets, Poetry for Physicists, and so on. Nearly every college has these courses; they are natural responses to consumer demand. Or they can take their three divisional courses in a single congenial specialty (three courses on music to satisfy the humanities requirement, or three courses in psychology to satisfy the natural science requirement). These may all be worthy courses, but they do not constitute breadth. Brown has no general education requirements at all, and this might be taken as recognition of the fact that students

---

as an SAT-II. Although these requirements are technically part of the general education curriculum, they are rarely subjects of controversy, in part because they are important mainly to the departments that staff them. There is no zero-sum interdepartmental gaming involved.

[3] Yale recently changed from a somewhat more elaborate distribution system. Unless otherwise cited, information about general education requirements is from college Web sites, and is subject to change.

will pursue their own interests no matter how ingenious the obstacle course, and that this pursuit is as likely as anything else is to give them breadth.[4]

Some colleges refine the categories or limit the number of courses that count toward satisfying their distribution requirements. The University of Virginia requires courses in each of five divisions of knowledge: social science, the humanities, historical studies, non-Western perspectives, and natural science, including mathematics. Princeton requires one or two courses in each of seven categories: epistemology and cognition, ethical thought and moral values, historical analysis, literature and the arts, quantitative reasoning, science and technology, and social analysis. Many colleges (Wesleyan is one) identify the courses in their catalogues that are considered appropriate for general education. The key element of any distribution system, though, is that the courses used to meet the requirements are departmental courses. The reason that distribution systems finesse the problem of devising and administering general education is that they leave the task of generating courses appropriate for the non-specialist up to departments. The theory is that departments have an incentive to offer such courses because they will enjoy increased enrollment, but there is rarely a penalty for ignoring the whole issue and letting students find their general education courses in the department next door.

The key element of the core model, on the other hand, is that all, or almost all, general education courses are extrade-

---

[4] Brown does require that its students demonstrate "competence in writing," but only students who instructors feel lack such competence are required to do course work addressing the problem.

partmental. These courses are designed specifically for non-specialists; they stand in a separate place in the catalogue; and they represent the things the faculty believes every educated person ought to know. These may be courses that all freshmen have to take—Pomona College, for example, requires an interdisciplinary Critical Inquiry Seminar in the first year (followed by a loosely constrained distribution requirement). Or it may be a full extradepartmental program, as it is at Columbia and Harvard.

A distribution system is cheaper and simpler to administer than a core program, and there are colleges that mix the two approaches.[5] But in their standard forms, the two systems reflect very different conceptions of what education essentially is. The idea behind a distribution system is that liberal learning is the sea in which the various departmentalized fields of study, from physics to poetry, all swim. Liberal education is not reducible to a specific body of knowledge. It's a background mentality, a way of thinking, a kind of intellectual DNA that informs work in every specialized area of inquiry. This DNA is what college tries to transmit. So that any liberal arts course that is properly taught will impart to the student, over and above specific information, a set of intellectual skills and attitudes, the acquisition of which constitutes what it means to be a liberally educated person. These skills and attitudes may change over time: for the last twenty years, for example, there has been an emphasis on "values" and "diversity," terms that were not heard much in the 1950s

---

[5] Stanford, for instance, has carefully circumscribed requirements in ethical reasoning, the global community, American cultures, and gender studies (all under the rubric of Education for Citizenship), in addition to an introductory humanities course and a "disciplinary breadth" requirement.

and 1960s, when "disinterestedness" and "science" were more prominent in definitions of liberal education. However it is defined, though, this mental disposition is the takeaway of the college experience. This is why, in a distribution system, it doesn't matter very much which courses students end up taking.

The idea behind core programs is that it does matter which courses students take, because there are certain things that they need to know. Columbia College believes that there are certain books that everyone ought to have read by the time they graduate. Harvard (under the program it has used since the late seventies) believes that there are certain methods of inquiry that students need to learn. At Columbia, not just any literature course will give students what they need; they must take Literature Humanities, which is a great books course. At Harvard, not just any history course will do; students must take a course that introduces them to the methods of historical analysis. Having a core program means believing that there is a discrete body of knowledge that constitutes a liberal education, and this is why some colleges go to the trouble of creating an extradepartmental roster of general education courses.

Where did the concept of general education come from? Requiring courses in prescribed subjects seems to belong to an ancient idea of learning, a holdover from the era of the pre-modern college, which was an institution in which almost everything students took was prescribed. But when almost everything is prescribed, there is no need for a concept like general education. General education is not a ghost from the past. It is a twentieth-century phenomenon, and it is, in some respects, the most modern part of the modern university. And it is just what is modern about general education that makes proposals for general education reform so difficult to negotiate.

General education was a response to the rise of the research university in the United States, between 1880 and 1920.[6] The research university is characterized by specialization. Its teachers are trained as specialists and its undergraduates are encouraged to follow their own interests by choosing a major field of study and then some number of electives from the other courses on offer in the catalogue. This kind of education attracted two types of critics, both of which are associated with the idea of general education.

The first type thought that education in the modern college was too narrow and utilitarian, that it led to pre-professionalization and overspecialization, a process unleavened by an ad hoc smattering of electives.[7] For these critics, general education became the name for whatever it was that a curriculum of majors and electives failed to provide, and it could be defined in various ways. (Arthur Levine, of Columbia Teachers College, lists a dozen meanings of the term "general education"

---

[6] The discussion of the history of general education reform in this chapter draws on a Harvard University document, "Curricular Renewal in Harvard College" (2006), to which I contributed in collaboration with a number of colleagues and administrators. The section I draw on was researched and drafted by me, but benefited from the editorial oversight of the entire committee. (This was an interim report and its recommendations were later superseded.)

[7] See Laurence R. Veysey, *The Emergence of the American University* (Chicago: University of Chicago Press, 1965), pp. 180–251; Julie A. Reuben, *The Making of the Modern University: Intellectual Transformation and the Marginalization of Morality* (Chicago: University of Chicago Press, 1996), esp. pp. 61–87; and Jon H. Roberts and James Turner, *The Sacred and the Secular University* (Princeton: Princeton University Press, 2000), pp. 83–106.

in his *Handbook on Undergraduate Curriculum*, published in
1978.)[8] Sometimes general education was imagined as what
turn-of-the-century educators called "liberal culture," a cul-
tivation of values distinct from, or opposed to, those of the
professions; sometimes it was moral philosophy, an attempt
to make up for the displacement of religion by science in the
modern university; sometimes it referred to what was per-
manent or universal in culture, to knowledge that transcends
specialized scholarship. All of these goals still cling to the
concept of general education today. They are behind the belief
that a college education should get at something bigger than
any single discipline, or even than any group of disciplines.

But it was the other type of criticism that led to the establishment of the two general education programs that served
as inspirations for many others, the programs at Columbia
and at Harvard. This second type of criticism was not that
the modern university was too utilitarian, too focused on the
ambition of "making it." It was that the modern college was
not worldly enough, and that devotion to knowledge for its
own sake led professors to neglect the socializing aspect of
what they were doing. The stories of the general education
programs at Columbia, beginning in 1919, and Harvard,
beginning in 1945, suggest that general education programs
are almost always motivated by what is going on in the world
outside the academy—and this is a case in which the excep-
tions, precisely because they are so self-consciously different,
tend to prove the rule. General education is where colleges
connect what professors do with who their students are and

[8] Arthur Levine, *Handbook on Undergraduate Curriculum* (San Francisco:
Jossey-Bass, 1978), pp. 3–4.

what they will become after they graduate—where colleges actually think about the outcome of the experience they provide. General education is, historically, the public face of liberal education.

3.

Columbia's famous general education courses are called Literature Humanities (officially, Masterpieces of European Literature and Philosophy; unofficially, Lit Hum) and Contemporary Civilization (officially, Contemporary Civilization in the West; unofficially, CC). The first is a year-long survey of Western literature starting with the *Iliad* and is required of all freshmen; the second is a year-long survey of moral and political thought from the Greeks to the twentieth century and is required of all sophomores. The syllabi have changed since the 1940s, when Literature Humanities was added to Contemporary Civilization as a requirement. Between 1940 and 1995, more than one hundred different books were taught in Literature Humanities. But the changes are relatively insignificant—one Shakespeare play or nineteenth-century novel for another. The basic impression is one of canonical stability.[9]

The courses arose independently. Contemporary Civilization began at the time of the First World War as a course

---

[9] As many commentators have remarked, it would be virtually impossible to get a faculty to agree on a single fixed syllabus for those (or nearly any other) subjects today; that the Columbia core is grandfathered in—that it has become the face of the franchise, so to speak—is possibly the main reason it still exists. Contemporary Civilization and Literature Humanities are only a part of Columbia's general education program.

called War Aims. It was taught by Frederick Woodbridge, a philosophy professor who was later dean of the graduate faculty, and it was part of a program designed at the request of the U.S. Army for students in the Student Army Training Corps (SATC). The SATC, the precursor of the ROTC, was a creation of the National Defense Act of 1916. Columbia's president, Nicholas Murray Butler, was a supporter of Woodrow Wilson's war policies—he had two professors dismissed for anti-draft activity—and War Aims was, as the university's historian, Robert McCaughey, puts it, "a course in Allied apologetics, with no pretense at objectivity or balance."[10]

After the armistice, Peace Aims was considered as a new title for the course, but Contemporary Civilization was chosen instead. Contemporary Civilization was a one-year course required of all freshmen. Its distinctive character—what made it a general education rather than departmental course—was the emphasis on the contemporary world. The syllabus for 1919 explained that "We are living in a world in which there are great and perplexing issues on which keen differences of opinion have arisen; and it is important now, not less than during the war, that men should understand the forces which

[10] Robert A. McCaughey, *Stand, Columbia: A History of Columbia University in the City of New York, 1754–2004* (New York: Columbia University Press, 2003), p. 290. On the development of the core curriculum at Columbia, see ibid., pp. 285–99, and Timothy P. Cross's history of the core (1995), at http://www.college.columbia.edu/core/oasis/history0.php. See also Justus Buchler, "Reconstruction in the Liberal Arts," in Dwight C. Miner, ed., *A History of Columbia College on Morningside* (New York: Columbia University Press, 1954), pp. 48–135; W. B. Carnochan, *The Battleground of the Curriculum: Liberal Education and American Experience* (Stanford: Stanford University Press, 1993), pp. 68–87; and Levine, *Handbook*, pp. 330–33.

are at work in the society of their own day."[11] In its first ten years, no material before 1871 was covered, and the students did not read primary historical texts; they used textbooks. In 1928, the economist Rexford Tugwell, who was the author of one of those textbooks, *American Economic Life and the Means of Its Improvement* (1925), persuaded the college to add a second full-year required course, called Today's Problems. (Tugwell left Columbia in 1933 to join the Roosevelt administration.) The extra year allowed the course to expand its historical coverage, but students did not read primary texts in Contemporary Civilization until after the Second World War. Today, the syllabus is all primary texts.

Columbia's curricular response to the First World War was not unique. Dartmouth and Stanford both instituted courses called Problems of Citizenship around the same time. Williams College created a course on American National Problems. These were all general education courses: they provided students with instruction in matters that fell outside the purview of departments, because they were either too broad or too current. The University of Missouri created a wartime course whose title is an unusually naked instance of pedagogical bundling: it was called Problems of American Citizenship, Including English Composition. The name of Stanford's Problems of Citizenship course was changed, after a little more than ten years, to Western Civilization.[12] The reason that colleges created required courses designed to introduce students to the political traditions of the West was, to use a word from another time, relevance. Colleges looked

[11] Quoted in Carnochan, *Battleground*, p. 76.

[12] Ibid., pp. 70–72.

at the world, and at what they perceived to be at stake in current events, and they decided that there were certain things students needed to know that most of them were not getting from specialized study.

The figure behind Columbia's Literature Humanities requirement was John Erskine, an English professor who was concerned about the fact that Columbia was attracting large numbers of students who were immigrants or the children of immigrants. He was particularly worried about Jewish students, and he proposed a course on "great Anglo-Saxon writers." The purpose of the course was socialization, not conversion. Erskine wanted to provide young people from different backgrounds with a common culture, something he thought was already thin in the United States.

The history of the course is tangled. Erskine proposed it before the war, but he was not given a chance to teach it until 1920, when it was offered as a two-year course known as General Honors. It was the first general education course in the humanities ever given in an American university, and it was a hit with the students. By 1925, there were eleven sections, most of them team-taught. In 1928, Erskine resigned. As advocates of general education curricula sometimes are, he was regarded as a dilettante by many of his colleagues. He had also published a bestselling potboiler, *The Private Life of Helen of Troy* (1925), and he left academia, to which his attachment had never been strong. The course was discontinued in 1929; but in 1932, it was revived by Jacques Barzun, a lecturer in the History department (and an alumnus of General Honors).

Barzun renamed it, charmingly, The Colloquium in Important Books, and in 1934 he invited Lionel Trilling, a graduate student and instructor in the English department, to teach it with him. Trilling, too, had been a student of Erskine's. He was the son of Jewish immigrants, and although he had been introduced to English literature at home (his mother was born in England), the course made a lasting impression on him.[13] The collaboration was a success, and Barzun and Trilling taught the course together, on and off, for thirty years. It remained an honors course (that is, enrollment was restricted), and it became one of the most famous courses in the history of the college. A faculty debate over whether to establish a similar course for all students was carried on for several years, until, in 1937, two courses, Humanities A, on Western literature, and Humanities B, on music and the arts, were introduced. Both were made requirements in 1947, the year that marks the start of the Humanities piece in Columbia's core curriculum.

The longevity of Columbia's general education program speaks for itself. Even so, the courses were opposed from the start by many members of the faculty; after 1945, and particularly after the sixties, staffing them was a problem. The faculty who taught them in the early years—Erskine, Barzun, Trilling, Tugwell, Clifton Fadiman, Joseph Wood Krutch,

---

[13] The course is the spine that runs through Trilling's literary criticism, from his first, enormously successful collection, *The Liberal Imagination* (1950), to his last book, *Sincerity and Authenticity* (1972), which is virtually a gloss on the syllabus. Trilling describes the course in some detail in "On the Teaching of Modern Literature," in his *Beyond Culture: Essays on Literature and Learning* (New York: Viking, 1965), pp. 3–30; he also comments on it in "Reflections on a Lost Cause: English Literature and American Education" (1958), in Diana Trilling, ed., *Speaking of Literature and Society* (New York: Harcourt Brace Jovanovich, 1980), pp. 243–69, and "Some Notes for an Autobiographical Lecture," in Diana Trilling, ed., *The Last Decade: Essays and Reviews, 1965–75* (New York: Harcourt Brace Jovanovich, 1979), pp. 231–34.

Mark Van Doren, Mortimer Adler—were public intellectuals. Colleagues who considered themselves to be more rigorous scholars condescended to them, and they returned the compliment. Medievalists in Romance language departments could not see what qualified a professor of Victorian literature, which is what Trilling was, to teach Dante. When Adler and Richard McKeon left Columbia for the University of Chicago, the general education curriculum they instituted there, under Chicago's president, Robert Maynard Hutchins, was far more canonical—more "great books"-oriented—than Columbia's. But even at Chicago, there was faculty resistance from specialists. This led two professors, Stringfellow Barr and Scott Buchanan, to leave Chicago for St. John's College, in Annapolis, where they established what is the purest of the great books curricula.[14]

Harvard's general education program also arose out of the experience of wartime. Though Harvard may seem, by virtue of its age and reputation, to represent a conservative and traditional model of higher education, and although it is certainly not a progressive school pedagogically, the university has often been in the forefront of educational change. Harvard has had some crusading presidents, and James Bryant Conant was one of them.

Conant was president of Harvard from 1933 to 1953. He was a "townie," from Dorchester, who had attended Harvard and joined the faculty in the Chemistry department. He was not an obvious choice to succeed Harvard's previous presi-

---

[14] Students at St. John's take a four-year seminar on classic texts in Western thought and literature (which includes, for seniors, four weeks on the writings of Karl Marx).

dent, A. Lawrence Lowell, a descendant of a famous Boston family. Conant had been passed over by his own high school, Roxbury Latin, in its search for a headmaster. But he became a force in American education and American government. The educational reform he is most closely associated with is the establishment of a meritocratic system in college admissions and faculty advancement. Under Conant, Harvard recruited and provided scholarships to students with high aptitude who otherwise could not have afforded to attend and would probably never have imagined applying; and it made publication a requirement for promotion, often obliging junior professors (by denying them tenure, which is the president's prerogative at Harvard) to leave for other universities so that they could produce sufficient scholarship to be hired back. He was a force behind both the widespread adoption of the Scholastic Aptitude Test (or SAT), which is basically an IQ test that is supposed to measure aptitude in a culturally neutral way, and the founding of the Educational Testing Service, which opened in 1948.[15]

In 1943, Conant appointed a committee of professors—including the historian Arthur Schlesinger, Sr.; the pioneer of

---

[15] See Nicholas Lemann, *The Big Test: The Secret History of the American Meritocracy* (New York: Farrar, Straus and Giroux, 1999), pp. 42–52, 78–79. James Hershberg's biography, *James B. Conant: Harvard to Hiroshima and the Making of the Nuclear Age* (New York: Knopf, 1993), is mostly concerned with Conant's involvement with the atomic bomb. (Conant served as chief civilian administrator of nuclear research during the war and was responsible for the recommendation—not the decision, which was the Secretary of War's—that the bomb be dropped on Hiroshima and Nagasaki.) Hershberg does not discuss Conant's educational reforms in much detail. I discuss both aspects of Conant's career in "The Long Shadow of James B. Conant," *American Studies* (New York: Farrar, Straus and Giroux, 2002), pp. 91–111.

modern English studies I. A. Richards; the classicist John H. Finley; and the biologist and future Nobel laureate George Wald; and chaired by the dean of the Faculty of Arts and Sciences, Paul Buck, a historian—and charged it with devising a curriculum that would give students, in Conant's words, "a common . . . understanding of the society which they will possess in common."[16] The committee met for two years, conducted extensive inquiries inside and outside Harvard, and, in 1945, published its report. This was *General Education in a Free Society*, a work sometimes referred to as the Harvard Report or, because of the crimson binding, the Redbook. The intended audience was national as well as intramural: the report discusses general education in high schools (something that is still the exception in writings on education, where K–12 is usually treated independently of tertiary education) and it analyzes the changes in American life that make general education important. It also recommends that Harvard adopt a general education system with courses in three areas: the humanities (a great books course); social science (also a "great texts"–based course); and natural science. The faculty voted to adopt this system. It had a three-year trial run, and became a requirement in 1950.

This was Harvard's first try at a general education program, and its fate was not as happy as Columbia's. But, regardless of its effect on undergraduate instruction at Harvard, the Red-

---

[16] Quoted in Morton Keller and Phyllis Keller, *Making Harvard Modern: The Rise of America's University*, 2nd ed. (New York: Oxford University Press, 2007), p. 44. On the Redbook and the fate of its general education program at Harvard, see ibid., pp. 42–46, and Phyllis Keller, *Getting at the Core: Curricular Reform at Harvard* (Cambridge, MA: Harvard University Press, 1982), pp. 10–18.

book mattered, for two reasons. The first was its success as a
book. It was widely read and widely discussed. By 1950, it
had sold more than 40,000 copies. It put general education
on the national map, much to the annoyance of Columbia—
an annoyance that persists to this day.[17] (But Columbia never
produced a manifesto.) The Redbook made colleges pay attention to the question of "what every student should know,"
whether those colleges ended up instituting full-fledged general education programs or not.

The other reason the Harvard Report mattered was its
rationale. *General Education in a Free Society* is a Cold War
document. Many of its conclusions are parallel to the ones
reached by President Truman's Commission on Higher Education, headed by the educator George Zook, whose report,
released in 1947, focuses explicitly on higher education as a
national resource.[18] Zook's report argued that investment in
higher education was crucial to the development of American
economic power. The Harvard authors were also concerned
about the nation's health. They identified two dangers in
postwar America. One was increasing socioeconomic diversity, the segregation of citizens according to income, which
is itself a function of educational attainment. Conant's committee was worried that this socioeconomic diversity (it did
not mention religious, racial, or other types of diversity) carried the risk of class resentment, as better-educated groups
acquired disproportionately greater wealth. This seemed

---

[17] See Cross, at http://www.columbia.edu/core/oasis/history0.php.

[18] *Higher Education for Democracy: A Report of the President's Commission on
Higher Education* (Washington, DC: U.S. Government Printing Office,
1947).

fertile ground for Marxists and other subversives. The other danger the report contemplated was intellectual relativism—a lack of commitment to a common set of beliefs, exacerbated by increased social mobility and the declining moral authority of traditional institutions, such as the church, the family, and the local community. Intellectual relativism made Americans susceptible to ideological indoctrination and fanaticism. Conant in particular believed that general education could help the United States withstand the threat of what he referred to as the "Russian hordes."[19] This is why the report devoted so many pages to general education in high schools. "General" really did mean everyone.

The authors felt that the most important effect of general education is that it gives students a "binding experience."[20] In a meritocratic society, citizens need a common fund of knowledge, a kind of cultural lingua franca, to prevent politically dangerous divisions from developing. In the Harvard model, the great books are not read because they articulate truths that transcend circumstances (though the members of the committee may have believed this as well). The great books are read because they have been read.[21] Whether Plato or

[19] Quoted in Hershberg, *James B. Conant*, p. 520.

[20] *General Education in a Free Society: Report of the Harvard Committee* (Cambridge, MA: Harvard University Press, 1945), p. 102.

[21] The alternative rationale is that the great books are timeless and should be taught for their own sake. This was the view of Robert Hutchins, who, with the help of Mortimer Adler, formerly at Columbia, instituted the famous great books program at the University of Chicago. See John W. Boyer, "A Twentieth-Century Cosmos: The New Plan and the Origins of General Education at Chicago," *University of Chicago Record*, 41 (January 18, 2007): 4–24. All general education programs are informed by a mix of these rationales—the material is important in its own right, but it is also important because it has been

Rousseau or Mill was right about fundamental human nature is not important; what is important is that we live in a society that is shaped to some degree by the ideas of Plato, Rousseau, and Mill, just as we live in a society in which we can expect to encounter works of literature influenced to some degree by Homer, Shakespeare, and Cervantes. Those writers are touchstones for contemporary culture and debate; more than that, they represent a common heritage that bonds each citizen, whether a lawyer or a cabdriver, to each. In the socioeconomically diverse world the Redbook imagines, in which cohorts divide off onto different educational paths as their talents and merits dictate, general education is the social glue.[22] At the start of the Cold War, Harvard did what Columbia had done at the time of the First World War: it supplemented its departmental curriculum with courses specially designed to meet contemporary exigencies. It put a public face on college education.

Conant was not entirely satisfied with his committee's rec-

---

important. The Chicago program was an extreme expression of the former theory—see Robert M. Hutchins, *The Higher Learning in America* (New Haven: Yale University Press, 1936). A recent incarnation of this split can be found in two books that rose to prominence simultaneously in 1987: Allan Bloom's *The Closing of the American Mind* and E. D. Hirsch's *Cultural Literacy*. Bloom, a Chicagoan, echoed Hutchins's claim for the timeless pedagogical relevance of the canonical works of Western philosophy. Hirsch, an English professor at the University of Virginia, argued for teaching the terms and phrases that every would-be educated person ought to know because every educated person does know them. Bloom wanted students to be cultured; Hirsch merely wanted them to be literate.

[22] In his autobiography, Conant says that he later decided that "a unified, coherent culture" is impossible in a democratic country and that "a pluralistic ideology must be the basis of a democracy." James B. Conant, *My Several Lives: Memoirs of a Social Inventor* (New York: Harper & Row, 1970), p. 366.

ommendations. He worried that general education could not be entrusted to specialists, and thought that a separate general education faculty should have been called for. It was not, and that failure proved to be the worm in Conant's apple. The program underwent what one of its historians calls "an almost satiric distortion of its objectives." It was gradually diluted by the inclusion of specialized courses; eventually, students were able to fulfill the requirements with courses such as Scandinavian Cinema, and by 1966, the program was effectively abandoned.[23] It took more than a decade for Harvard to design and implement another general education curriculum. Reviving general education was difficult in part because academic life in the sixties was not friendly to concepts like consensus and the canon. But it was also difficult because general education programs tend to trigger the liberal arts college's autoimmune system. To understand why this is so, we need to go back to another educational crusader, Charles William Eliot.

4.

Eliot became president of Harvard in 1869. His academic field was chemistry, but (unlike his successor Conant) he was not a particularly accomplished chemist. In fact, he had resigned from the Harvard faculty, in 1863, after being passed over for a new chair. He left for Europe, where he spent two years inspecting educational systems in various countries. In 1865, he returned to the United States to take a position as professor of chemistry at the Massachusetts Institute of Technology, which had just been founded in Boston as a school

[23] Keller, *Getting to the Core*, pp. 17–19.

to prepare students for the scientific professions. When the Harvard Overseers chose Eliot, who was working at what many would have regarded as a vocational school, they were taking a radical step. His appointment constituted recognition that American higher education was changing, and that Harvard was in danger of losing its prestige. Harvard picked Eliot because it wanted to be reformed. Eliot did not disappoint. He was inaugurated in the fall of 1869 and he served for forty years.[24]

By the time he retired, Eliot had become identified with almost everything that distinguishes the modern research university from the antebellum college: the abandonment of the role of *in loco parentis*; the abolition of required coursework; the introduction of the elective system for undergraduates; the establishment of graduate schools with doctoral programs in the arts and sciences; and the emergence of pure and applied research as principal components of the university's mission. Eliot played a prominent part in all these developments. He was, after all, a prominent figure at a prominent school. But he was not their originator. Other colleges instituted many of these reforms well before Harvard did. Yale had been awarding doctorates since 1861, for example, and the trend toward applied research was kicked off by the Morrill Land-Grant College Act, passed by the wartime Congress in 1862. The

---

[24] On Eliot's reforms and their national importance, see Hugh Hawkins, *Between Harvard and America: The Educational Leadership of Charles W. Eliot* (New York: Oxford University Press, 1972). See also, on Eliot's presidency, Henry James, *Charles W. Eliot: President of Harvard University, 1869–1909* (Boston: Houghton Mifflin, 1930), vol. 1, esp. pp. 184–301, and Samuel Eliot Morison, *Three Centuries of Harvard, 1636–1936* (Cambridge, MA: Harvard University Press, 1936), pp. 323–64.

reform Eliot was most closely associated with was the elective system: by 1899 he had got rid of all required courses for Harvard undergraduates except first-year English and a foreign language requirement. Cornell and Brown, though, had tried free elective curricula well before Eliot. (Until his appointment, Eliot had actually been somewhat dubious of electives; he seems to have changed his mind, partly because of his own reflections on the advantages of an elective system, but possibly because a committee of the Harvard Overseers had drawn up a report recommending more of them before he was hired.)[25]

So Eliot's role was to some extent reactive. He was a quick student of trends and an aggressive implementer of change. He adopted a "new sheriff in town" manner toward his faculty (a manner that has not always proved effective at Harvard). But he did bring one original and revolutionary idea with him when he came into office. This was to make the bachelor's degree a prerequisite for admission to professional school. It may seem a minor reform, but it was possibly the key element in the transformation of American higher education in the decades after the Civil War.

Before Eliot, students entering higher education could choose between college and professional school—law, medicine, or science, which in the nineteenth century was taught at a school separate from the college. In 1869, Eliot's first year as president, half of the students at Harvard Law School and nearly three quarters of the students at Harvard Medical School had not attended college and did not hold undergraduate degrees. These were, comparatively, respectable numbers.

[25] Hawkins, *Between Harvard and America*, pp. 92–93.

Only 19 of the 411 medical students at the University of Michigan, and none of the 387 law students there, had prior degrees of any kind. There were no admissions requirements at Harvard Law School, beyond evidence of "good character" and the ability to pay the hundred dollars tuition, which went into the pockets of the law professors. There were no grades or exams, and students often left before the end of the two-year curriculum to go to work. They received their degrees on schedule anyway. Standards at medical schools were only a little less amorphous. To get an MD at Harvard, students were obliged to take a ninety-minute oral examination, during which nine students rotated among nine professors, all sitting in one large room, spending ten minutes with each. When the ninety minutes were up, a bell was sounded, and the professors, without consulting one another, marked pass or fail for their fields on a chalkboard. Any student who passed five of the nine fields became a doctor.

Eliot considered the situation scandalous. He published an article about it in *The Atlantic Monthly* in 1869, just a few months before being offered the presidency, and that article was almost certainly a factor in the decision to appoint him. Harvard wanted a reformer because there was alarming evidence in the 1860s that college enrollments were in decline in the United States, and the existence of an easy professional school option was one of the reasons why. Once installed, Eliot immediately set about instituting admission and graduation requirements at Harvard's schools of medicine, law, divinity, and science, and forcing those schools to develop meaningful curricula. It took some time: a bachelor's degree was not required for admission to the Harvard Medical School until 1900.

Eliot's reform had several long-term effects on American education and American society. First, it professionalized the professions. It erected a hurdle on what had been a fairly smooth path, compelling future doctors and lawyers to commit to four years of liberal arts education before entering what are, essentially, professional certification programs. This made the professions more selective and thereby raised the social status of law, medicine, and science and engineering. Law students were no longer teenagers looking for a shortcut to a comfortable career; they were college graduates, required to demonstrate that they had acquired specific kinds of knowledge. People who couldn't clear the hurdles couldn't advance to practice. Eliot's reform helped put universities in the exclusive business of credentialing professionals.

The emergence of pure research as part of the university's mission—the notion that professors should be paid to produce work that might have no practical application—was the nineteenth-century development that Eliot had least enthusiasm for. He believed in the importance of undergraduate teaching—as a champion of electives, he always insisted that the subject was less important than the teacher—and he believed in the social value of professional schools. But he was too committed to the doctrine of laissez-faire to believe in research whose worth could not be measured in the marketplace, and Harvard did not formally establish a graduate school in arts and sciences until 1890, rather late in the history of graduate education. The push toward doctoral-level education came from elsewhere.

Still, as Eliot quickly realized, graduate schools perform the same function as professional schools. Doctoral programs, and the requirement that college teachers hold a PhD, professionalized the professoriate. The standards for scholarship, like the standards for law and medicine, became systematized: everyone had to clear the same hurdles and to demonstrate competence in a scholarly specialty. People who could not clear the hurdles, or who had never joined the race, were pushed to the margins of their fields. The late nineteenth-century university was really (to adopt a mid-twentieth-century term) a multiversity—it had far less coherence than the antebellum college, since it was essentially a conglomeration of non-overlapping specialties. It altered the intellectual environment, and not every organism proved able to adapt.

Eliot's reform saved the liberal arts college from drowning in an increasingly mass, mobile, and materialistic society. In 1870, one out of every sixty men between eighteen and twenty-one years old was a college student; by 1900, one out of every twenty-five was in college.[26] Eliot was a Brahmin of the Brahmins. His father, Samuel A. Eliot, was a graduate of the Harvard Divinity School, a mayor of Boston, a one-term congressman, and one of the richest men in Massachusetts before he lost everything in the financial panic of 1857. But Eliot did not see the function of institutions such as Harvard to be that of perpetuating existing hierarchies of wealth and class. He understood that in an expanding nation, social and economic power would pass to people who, regardless of birth and inheritance, possessed specialized expertise. If a

---

[26] In 1940, it was one out of every 6.5. See Burton J. Bledstein, *The Culture of Professionalism: The Middle Class and the Development of Higher Education in America* (New York: W. W. Norton, 1976), p. 278. Today, half of all Americans have some experience of college; 25 percent earn college degrees (associate's or bachelor's).

liberal arts education remained an optional luxury for these people, then the college would wither away.

By making college the gateway to the professions, Eliot linked the college to the rising fortunes of this new professional class. But he also enabled the college to preserve its anti-utilitarian ethos in an increasingly secular and utilitarian age. For Eliot insisted on keeping liberal education separate from professional and vocational education. He thought that utility should be stressed everywhere in the professional schools but nowhere in the colleges. The collegiate ideal, he explained in his *Atlantic Monthly* article, is "the enthusiastic study of subjects for the love of them without any ulterior objects."[27] College is about knowledge for its own sake—hence the free elective system, which let students roam across the curriculum without being shackled to the requirements of a major. And this is the system we have inherited: liberalization first, then professionalization. The two types of education are kept separate.

Eliot's reform left a question mark in the undergraduate experience. What, if nothing they were learning was intended to have real-world utility, were undergraduates supposed to learn? The free election system basically said, It doesn't matter; you will learn what you really need to know in graduate school. And abuses of the system, a problem that was much debated in higher education circles in the late nineteenth century, led to a reaction against it after the turn of the century.[28] But the idea that liberal arts education is by its nature divorced from professional education persisted. This separation is one of the

---

[27] Quoted in Hawkins, *Between Harvard and America*, p. 105.

[28] Veysey, *The Emergence of the American University*, pp. 248–59.

chief characteristics of elite institutions of higher learning, and it is the buried assumption in the resistance to general education programs that undertake to connect what undergraduates learn with the world outside the academy. In a system that associates college with the ideals of the love of learning and knowledge for its own sake, a curriculum designed with real-world goals in mind can seem utilitarian, instrumentalist, vocational, presentist, anti-intellectual—illiberal.

5.

Professors still tend to feel that there are things that every educated person should know, and one means of accommodating this mission without arousing the autoimmune system is to define general education as an introduction to scholarly methods. This is what Harvard did in the 1970s, under its president, Derek Bok, and his dean, Henry Rosofsky, when the faculty created and adopted the Core. The Core is a program with eleven course categories, from literature and moral reasoning to historical study and physical science. The courses are almost all extradepartmental; they stand in a separate place in the catalogue. Students need to take seven (from which categories depends on their major field) to graduate. This is a system that no longer draws a bright line between what goes on in the academic disciplines and what goes on in general education classes. It allows professors to teach their specialties, since the takeaway is a method of inquiry rather than wide knowledge of a subject. Courses can, in other words, be quite narrowly focused (Scandinavian Cinema) and still accomplish the assigned mission.

The Core program, like most of its predecessors in American higher education, was designed with a view to preparing students for life after college. Though the courses were on the usual subject matters of the disciplines, the Core was not about learning for its own sake. It was about learning how to learn. When the program was being designed, Rosofsky is supposed to have decreed that the Harvard faculty would not shed blood over books—meaning that there would be no attempt to impose a canon.[29] The emphasis on the traditional disciplines avoided the danger of political warfare that loomed over any curricular reform in the aftermath of the sixties. The very idea of requirements was inconsistent with the spirit of the age. At Stanford in 1968, a committee appointed to look into curricular reform by the university's president, J. E. Wallace Sterling, and chaired by its vice-provost, Herbert L. Packer, concluded that "the faculty member should be free to pursue his intellectual interests wherever they lead him. The student, other things being equal, should be equally free." The committee found that "the general educational ideal is totally impracticable as a dominant curricular pattern in the modern university."[30]

In making the move from subject matter to methods, Harvard was being consistent with trends at other institutions. Brown introduced optional Modes of Thought courses in 1969, designed to "place major emphasis on the methods, concepts and value systems required in approaching an understanding of a specific problem, topic, or issue in a particular field of inquiry." In 1974, the University of Michigan provided, as part of its general education program, an Approaches to

[29] The history of the creation of Harvard's Core curriculum is in Keller's *Getting to the Core*.

[30] Quoted in Carnochan, *Battleground*, pp. 97–98.

Knowledge curriculum that specified four approaches: analytical, empirical, moral, and aesthetic.[31] But the post-sixties norm was the distribution system. In 1976, about 7 percent of American liberal arts colleges had core general education programs—defined as programs in which students took the same courses or read the same books. Almost 90 percent of liberal arts colleges had a distribution system, in some of which a distribution of courses was merely recommended.[32] It was not a climate favorable to prescriptivism.

In the last ten years, though, there has been a swing back toward requirements and the idea of general education. When Harvard revisited its Core program in 2004, a committee of professors recommended switching to distribution requirements, and the faculty rejected the proposal. No one thought that what students needed to know was self-evident, but most professors felt that whatever it was, the college had an obligation to give it to them. Where the process tended to run into difficulties was where general education proposals have always encountered friction—not only with the problem of specialists teaching non-specialists, but with the problem of recasting liberal education with life goals in mind.

6.

Was Eliot's segregation of liberal arts education from the professional schools a devil's bargain? By erecting a wall

[31] Carnegie Foundation for the Advancement of Teaching, *Missions of the College Curriculum: A Contemporary Review with Suggestions* (San Francisco: Jossey-Bass, 1977), pp. 171–72.

[32] Levine, *Handbook*, pp. 10–14.

between the liberal arts and the professions, it gave colleges an allergy to the term "vocational." That word is heard a lot from critics of general education proposals, along with words like "presentist" and "instrumentalist." There is a little self-deception in the complaints about vocationalism, since there is one vocation, after all, for which a liberal arts education is not only useful but deliberately designed: the vocation of professor. The undergraduate major is essentially a preparation for graduate work in the field, which leads to a professional position. The major is set up in such a way that the students who receive the top marks are the ones who show the greatest likelihood of going on to graduate school and becoming professors themselves. And it seems strange to accuse any educational program of being instrumentalist. Knowledge just *is* instrumental: it puts us into a different relationship with the world. The accusation of presentism is the telling one, though; for it has been in response to present circumstances that the most ambitious general education programs have, historically, been introduced. It's what is going on in the present that makes colleges need continually to redefine what they do. Are we preparing our students for the world they are about to confront? is the question that colleges ask. If the faculty thinks that a curriculum in which students spend most of four years being trained in an academic specialty is not going to do it, then general education is the answer.

The danger that faces liberal education today is the same as the danger that it faced in Eliot's day: that it will be marginalized by the proliferation, and the attraction, of non-liberal alternatives. There are data to support this anxiety. Most of the roughly 2,500 four-year colleges in the United States award less than half of their degrees in the liberal arts. Even in the leading research universities, only about half the bachelor's degrees are awarded in liberal arts fields.[33] The biggest undergraduate major by far in the United States is business. Twenty-two percent of all bachelor's degrees are awarded in that field. Ten percent of all bachelor's degrees are awarded in education. Seven percent are awarded in the health professions. Those are not liberal arts fields. There are almost twice as many bachelor's degrees conferred every year in social work as there are in all foreign languages and literatures combined. Only 4 percent of college graduates major in English. Just 2 percent major in history.[34] In fact, the proportion of undergraduate degrees awarded annually in the liberal arts and sciences has been declining for a hundred years, apart from a brief rise between 1955 and 1970, which was a period of rapidly increasing enrollments and national economic growth.[35] Except for those fifteen unusual years, the more American

[33] About a third of four-year colleges in the United States have curricula that concentrate on liberal arts and sciences or that balance liberal arts and preprofessional coursework—see "Undergraduate Instructional Program: Distribution of institutions and enrollments by classification category," Carnegie Foundation for the Advancement of Teaching. Several years ago, in light of the increasingly mixed nature of undergraduate curricula in American colleges, the Carnegie Foundation dropped "liberal arts and sciences" as a stand-alone designation from its classificatory scheme. Most Americans who attend college do not have a liberal arts education.

[34] Bachelor's degrees conferred by degree-granting institutions, by discipline division, *Digest of Education Statistics*.

[35] Joan Gilbert, "The Liberal Arts College: Is It Really an Endangered Species?," *Change*, 27 (September–October 1995): 36. Gilbert detected a swing upward in the percentage of liberal arts degrees in the eighties, but an analysis of degrees awarded since 1972 suggests that, both proportionately and in absolute numbers, the underlying trend is downwards.

higher education has expanded, the more the liberal arts sector has shrunk in proportion to the whole.

The instinctive response of liberal educators is to pull up the drawbridge, to preserve college's separateness at any price. But maybe purity is the disease. What are the liberal arts and sciences? They are simply fields in which knowledge is pursued disinterestedly—that is, without regard to political, economic, or practical benefit. Disinterestedness doesn't mean that the professor is equally open to any view. Professors are hired because they have views about their subjects, views that exclude opposing or alternative views. Disinterestedness just means that whatever views a professor does hold, they have been arrived at unconstrained, or as unconstrained as possible, by anything except the requirement of honesty.

Almost any liberal arts field can be made non-liberal by turning it in the direction of some practical skill with which it is already associated. English departments can become writing programs, even publishing programs; pure mathematics can become applied mathematics, even engineering; sociology shades into social work; biology shades into medicine; political science and social theory lead to law and political administration; and so on. But conversely, and more importantly, any practical field can be made liberal simply by teaching it historically or theoretically. Many economics departments refuse to offer courses in accounting, despite student demand for them. It is felt that accounting is not a liberal art. Maybe not, but one must always remember the immortal dictum: Garbage is garbage, but the *history* of garbage is scholarship. Accounting is a trade, but the *history* of accounting is a subject of disinterested inquiry—a liberal art. And the accountant who knows something about the history of accounting will be a better accountant. That knowledge pays off in the marketplace. Similarly, future lawyers benefit from learning about the philosophical aspects of the law, just as literature majors learn more about poetry by writing poems.

This gives a clue to the value-added potential of liberal education. Historical and theoretical knowledge, which is the kind of knowledge that liberal education disseminates, is knowledge that exposes the contingency of present arrangements. It unearths the a prioris buried in present assumptions; it shows students the man behind the curtain; it provides a glimpse of what is outside the box. It encourages students to think for themselves. Liberal educators know this, but sometimes they make the wrong inference. They think that showing the man behind the curtain subverts the spectacle. But merely revealing the contingency and constructedness of present arrangements does not end the spectacle, and subversiveness is not the point. The spectacle goes on. The goal of teaching students to think for themselves is not an empty sense of self-satisfaction. The goal is to enable students, after they leave college, to make more enlightened contributions to the common good.

It's sometimes claimed that learning any scholarly field well develops general mental faculties, which may then be applied to problems and issues encountered in life after college. But problems and issues in the academic world are not always analogous to problems and issues in the non-academic world; resolving problems and issues in the non-academic world usually requires taking into account frictions of a kind deliberately bracketed in the academy. And the vast majority of college graduates today will seek work well outside the academic band of the occupational spectrum. Even at Harvard, where students are supposed to be trained at the cutting edges of the academic disciplines, less than 10 percent of graduates pursue a PhD. More than 50 percent pursue careers in law, medicine, and business. What relevant knowledge and skills does college provide these students with? That is the question a general education needs to answer.

In the system that Eliot helped to bring into being, professional education is the monopoly of the professional schools. Only lawyers get to teach the law to future lawyers. In most liberal arts colleges, students cannot take a course on the law (apart from the occasional legal history course). Many students in liberal arts colleges never take a class in business, or even in economics. Most take no classes in architecture, education, or engineering, unless they are in a special, and usually segregated, program. Few students who do not intend to become specialists take courses in subjects touching on health or technology. These are matters that everyone has to deal with in life, and knowing something about them is important to being able to participate effectively in the political process. But college graduates typically have no more sophisticated an understanding of them than people who have attended only high school do. The divorce between liberalism and professionalism as educational missions rests on a superstition: that the practical is the enemy of the true. This is nonsense. Disinterestedness is perfectly consistent with practical ambition, and practical ambitions are perfectly consistent with disinterestedness. If anyone should understand that, it's a college professor.

2

The Humanities Revolution

1.

ABOUT TWENTY YEARS ago, the humanities acquired a rationale problem.[1] In sociological terms, they suffered an institutional legitimacy crisis. A public perception arose that study and teaching in fields such as literature and art history had gotten off track. The problem was not that humanists were unable to provide rationales for their work; many did.[2]

[1] The humanities are one of (usually) three liberal arts divisions; they are defined differently at different institutions, and there are many possible subfields within a humanities division. Harvard has more than twenty degree programs in the humanities. A principal difference among institutions is whether history is counted as a humanities discipline (as it is at Yale) or a social science (as it is at Harvard). Changes in the study and teaching of history were very much part of the public debate over the condition of the humanities, less so in the internal debates. Philosophy largely escaped attention, both internally and externally.

[2] See, among others, George Levine et al., *Speaking for the Humanities* (New York: American Council of Learned Societies, 1989); Michael Bérubé and Cary Nelson, eds., *Higher Education Under Fire: Politics, Economics, and the Crisis of the Humanities* (New York: Routledge, 1995); Martha Nussbaum, *Cultivating Humanity: A Classical Defense of Reform in Liberal Education* (Cambridge, MA: Harvard University Press, 1997); Sander Gilman, *The Fortunes of the Humanities: Thoughts for After the Year 2000* (Stanford: Stanford University Press, 2000); and Marjorie Garber, *A Manifesto for Literary Studies* (Seattle: Walter Chapin Simpson Center for the Humanities, 2003). See, in addi-

61

The problem was that even humanists felt that those rationales were not completely persuasive to outsiders—to the
public, to university administrators, and even to colleagues in
other academic disciplines. To some extent, the difficulty was
understandable. Disciplines are rarely called upon to justify
themselves. No one says, I don't understand a tenth of what
physics professors are talking about. Why should we spend
all this money on physics departments? The inaccessibility
of physics is built into the rationale for physics departments;
that is, we need physics departments precisely because special
training is necessary to teach and do research in physics. And
to most non-physicists, the value of doing physics goes without saying. People feel, out of ignorance or not, that there is
a good return on investment in physics departments. In the
1980s, people began wondering what the return on investment was in the humanities.

This skepticism produced some defensiveness on the part of
humanities professors, and it also led to a fair amount of self-
examination. Self-examination is usually a good thing, but it
can become obsessive, and the focus of humanities professors
on questions like "What's happened to the humanities?"[3] and
"Have the humanistic disciplines collapsed?"[4] did become a
little obsessive. There are fewer students majoring in humanities fields than was once the case, but undergraduates con-

---

tion, the mission statements of the many college and university Humanities
Centers that have been founded since the 1970s. A national Consortium of
Humanities Centers and Institutes was established in 1988.

[3] Alvin Kernan, ed., *What's Happened to the Humanities?* (Princeton: Princeton
University Press, 1997).

[4] The title of a conference held at the Stanford Humanities Center in 1999.

tinue to take courses in literature, art, music, and philosophy; despite an uncertain job market, people continue to apply to doctoral programs in those fields; and a great deal of scholarship continues to get published. The humanities disciplines may go through a period of reorganization, but they aren't likely to become extinct.

There was something slightly disproportionate about the reaction of humanists to questions about the value of the humanities. In literary terms, their response lacked an objective correlative.[5] In psychiatric terms, it was neurotic. There was anxiety that behind the problem of public justification was another problem, which was that professors in the humanities could not seem to produce a consensus around a paradigm for humanistic studies. It was not that humanists were quarreling with one another: that would only have meant that there were competing paradigms in the humanities fields, which is a sign of life. What was worrisome was that even in the absence of a quarrel, there was no clear agreement on a definition of what humanists do. Which raises the question, Does there need to be a definition? What is the history of the humanities disciplines that made the lack of a paradigm seem something like a crisis?

2.

The history of higher education in the United States since the Second World War can be divided into two periods. The

[5] T. S. Eliot, "Hamlet and His Problems," *The Sacred Wood* (London: Methuen, 1920), p. 100. In literature, the term "objective correlative" refers to an "exact equivalence" between a plot situation, or an image, and the emotion that the writer intends to evoke.

first period, from 1945 to 1975, was a time of expansion. The composition of the higher education system remained more or less the same—in some respects, the system became more uniform—but the size of the system increased dramatically. This is the period known in the literature on American education as the Golden Age. The second period, from 1975 to the present, has not been honored with a special name. It is an equally dramatic time, though, a period not of expansion but of diversification. Since 1975, the size of the system has grown at a much more modest pace, but the composition of the system—who is being taught, who does the teaching, and what they teach—has been transformed. It was a decade or so into the second phase, the period of diversification, that questions about the value of the humanities started being asked. But we cannot understand the second phase unless we understand the first.

In the Golden Age, between 1945 and 1975, the number of American undergraduates increased by almost 500 percent and the number of graduate students increased by nearly 900 percent.[6] Those are unprecedented and almost certainly unrepeatable figures. The rate of growth was nearly fantastic. In the sixties alone, undergraduate enrollments more than doubled, from 3.5 million to just under 8 million; the number of doctorates awarded every year tripled; and more faculty were hired than had been hired in the entire 325 years of

---

[6] Roger L. Geiger, "The Ten Generations of American Higher Education," in Philip G. Altbach, Robert O. Berdahl, and Patricia J. Gumport, eds., *American Higher Education in the Twenty-first Century: Social, Political, and Economic Challenges* (Baltimore: Johns Hopkins University Press, 1999), p. 61.

American higher education prior to 1960.[7] At the height of the expansion, between 1965 and 1972, new community college campuses were opening in the United States at the rate of one every week.[8]

Three factors account for this expansion. The first was the baby boom; the second was the relatively high domestic economic growth rate after 1948; and the third was the Cold War. What is sometimes forgotten about the baby boom is that it was a period of record high birth rates that followed a period of record low birth rates, the years of the Depression and the Second World War.[9] When Americans began, after 1945, reproducing at a rate that would exceed 4 million births a year, it was a sharp spike on the chart. The system had grown accustomed to abnormally small cohorts. A lot of slots had to be manufactured very quickly.

The role played by the Cold War in the expansion of higher education is well known. The American university had been drawn into the business of government-related scientific research during the Second World War by men like James Conant, president of Harvard, and Vannevar Bush. Bush, former vice president and dean of engineering at the Massachusetts Institute of Technology, was the director of the

---

[7] U.S. Bureau of the Census, *Historical Statistics of the United States, Colonial Times to 1970* (Washington, DC: U.S. Government Printing Office, 1975), Vol. 1, pp. 382, 387; Walter P. Metzger, "The Academic Profession in the United States," in Burton R. Clark, ed., *The Academic Profession: National, Disciplinary, and Institutional Settings* (Berkeley: University of California Press, 1987), p. 124.

[8] Geiger, "Ten Generations," p. 62.

[9] The birth rate in 1939 was 18.8 per 1,000 of population; in 1949, it was 24.5, almost a third again as high.

government Office of Scientific Research and Development during the war. At the time of the First World War, scientific research for military purposes had been carried out by military personnel, so-called soldier-scientists. It was Bush's idea to contract this work out to research universities, scientific institutes, and independent private laboratories instead. In 1945, he organized the publication of a report, *Science— The Endless Frontier,* which became the standard argument for government subvention of basic science in peacetime, and which launched the collaboration between American universities and the national government. Bush is the godfather of the system known as contract overhead—the practice of billing granting agencies for indirect costs, an idea that allowed universities to spread the wealth across all of its activities. This was the start of the gravy train that produced the Golden Age.[10]

Then, in 1957, came Sputnik. Although it had the size and lethal potential of a beach ball, Sputnik stirred up a panic in the United States. (It wasn't the satellite that caused the panic, of course; it was the missile used to launch it.) Among the responses was the passage of the National Defense Education Act of 1958. The act put the federal government, for the first time, in the business of subsidizing higher education directly, rather than through contracts for specific research.

---

[10] U.S. Office of Scientific Research and Development, *Science—The Endless Frontier* (Washington, DC: U.S. Government Printing Office, 1945). See Roger L. Geiger, *Research and Relevant Knowledge: American Research Universities Since World War II* (New York: Oxford University Press, 1993), pp. 157–97, and Hugh Davis Graham and Nancy Diamond, *The Rise of American Research Universities: Elites and Challengers in the Postwar Era* (Baltimore: Johns Hopkins University Press, 1997), pp. 26–50.

Before 1958, public support for higher education had been administered at the state level (which is one reason why there are state universities in the United States but no national university). After the passage of the National Defense Education Act, the main spigots from which government largesse flowed moved from the Department of Defense (which continued to be a major source of funding) to civilian agencies, notably the National Aeronautics and Space Administration, the National Science Foundation, and the National Institutes of Health. The act singled out two areas in particular as targets of public investment: science and foreign languages, thus pumping up two distinct areas of the academic system.

This was also the period, after Sputnik, when economists such as Gary Becker and Theodore Schultz introduced the concept of human capital,[11] which, by figuring educated citizens as a strategic resource, offered another national security rationale for government investment in higher education. In the words of the enabling legislation for the National Defense Education Act itself: "The security of the Nation requires the fullest development of the mental resources and technical skills of its young men and women. . . . We must increase our efforts to identify and educate more of the talent of our Nation. This requires programs that will give assurance that no students of ability will be denied an opportunity for

---

[11] Gary S. Becker, *Human Capital: A Theoretical and Empirical Analysis, with Special Reference to Education* (New York: National Bureau of Economic Research, 1964), and Theodore William Schultz, *The Economic Value of Education* (New York: Columbia University Press, 1963).

higher education because of financial need."[12] This was one of the triggers for the accelerated expansion of the 1960s.

The baby boom was another. The National Defense Education Act was passed just before the effects of the higher birth rate kicked in. Between 1955 and 1970, the number of eighteen- to twenty-four-year-olds in the United States grew from 15 million to 25 million.[13] The expansion received a late and unintentional boost from the military draft, which provided a deferment for college students until 1970. The result was that by 1968, more than 63 percent of male high school graduates were going on to college, a higher proportion than do today.[14] This is the period when all those community college campuses were springing up. They were, among other things, government-subsidized draft havens.

Then, around 1975, the Golden Age came to a halt. The student deferment was abolished and the Vietnam War ended; the college-age population leveled off; the country went into a recession; and the economic value of a college degree began to fall. In the seventies, the income differential between college graduates and high school graduates dropped from 61 percent to 48 percent.[15] The percentage of people going on to

---

[12] Quoted in Elizabeth A. Duffy and Idana Goldberg, *Crafting a Class: College Admissions and Financial Aid, 1955–1994* (Princeton: Princeton University Press, 1998), p. 170.

[13] Ibid., p. 4.

[14] College enrollment of recent high school graduates: 1960 to 1994, U.S. Bureau of the Census, *Statistical Abstract of the United States* (Washington, DC: U.S. Government Printing Office, 1996), p. 180.

[15] Duffy and Goldberg, *Crafting a Class*, p. 22. See also Marvin Lazerson, "The Disappointments of Success: Higher Education After World War II," *Annals of the American Academy of Political and Social Science*, 559 (1998): 72.

college therefore began to drop as well, and a system that had more than quintupled in size in the span of a single generation suddenly found itself with empty dormitory beds and a huge tenured faculty. This was the beginning of the long-term job crisis for American PhDs, and it was also the beginning of serious economic pressures on the liberal arts college.

Pressure on the liberal arts college translates into pressure on the humanities disciplines, because research in the humanities is essentially a by-product of the production of college teachers. The system produces professors; professors produce research. When the demand for college teachers drops, the resources available for research drop as well. From 1955 to 1970, the proportion of liberal arts degrees among all bachelor's degrees awarded annually had risen for the first time since 1900; after 1970, it began going down again.[16] Today, a third of all bachelor's degrees awarded annually in the United States are in the liberal arts, and less than 10 percent are in the humanities.[17]

American higher education did grow after 1975, but much more slowly, at a rate averaging about 1 percent a year. And it changed, but in a different way: it diversified. In 1947, 71 percent of college students in America were men; today, a

---

[16] Joan Gilbert, "The Liberal Arts College: Is It Really an Endangered Species?," *Change*, 27 (September–October 1995): 36–43.

[17] Bachelor's degrees earned by field: 1960 to 2006, *Digest of Education Statistics*. The figure for humanities degrees does not include history. If subjects such as religious vocation, area studies, general studies, and visual and performing arts are included, then the humanities account for 17 percent of all bachelor's degrees. See bachelor's and master's degrees conferred by degree-granting institutions, by field of study and state or jurisdiction: 2005–06, *Digest of Education Statistics*.

minority of college students—42 percent—are men.[18] As late as 1965, 94 percent of college students were classified as white; today, the figure for non-Hispanic whites is 66 percent.[19] Much of this diversification happened after the Golden Age, and a single statistic makes the point. In the decade between 1984 and 1994, the total enrollment in American colleges and universities increased by 2 million, but not one of those 2 million new students was a white American-born male. They were all non-whites, women, and foreign students. The number of white American men in American higher education actually declined between 1984 and 1994.[20]

Faculty demographics changed in the same way, a reflection not so much of changes in hiring practices as of demographic changes in the group that went to graduate school after 1975. In 1998, American faculty who had been hired before 1985 were 28 percent female and about 11 percent non-white or Hispanic. Full-time faculty hired after 1985—that is, for the most part, faculty who entered graduate school after the Golden Age—were 40 percent female and 18 percent non-

---

[18] "Today" means 2005, the latest year for which these breakdowns are available. The percentages of white students in undergraduate and graduate enrollments are the same. Total fall enrollment in degree-granting institutions, by attendance status, sex of student, and control of institution: Selected years, 1947 through 2005, *Digest of Education Statistics.*

[19] Total fall enrollment in degree-granting institutions, by race/ethnicity, sex, attendance status, and level of student: Selected years, 1976 through 2005, *Digest of Education Statistics.*

[20] Louis Menand, "Everyone Else's Higher Education," *New York Times Magazine,* April 20, 1997, p. 48. The statistic was calculated from tables in the *Chronicle of Higher Education,* Almanac Issue, 1996.

white.[21] These figures apply only to full-time professors; they do not include part-time faculty, who by 1998 constituted 40 percent of the teaching force in American higher education, and who were more likely than full-time faculty to be female.[22] In 1997, 45,394 doctoral degrees were conferred in the United States; 40 percent of the recipients were women (in the arts and humanities, just under 50 percent were women), and only 63 percent were classified as white American citizens. The other 37 percent were non-white Americans and foreign students.[23] The demographic mix in higher education, including both students and faculty, changed dramatically in the span of twenty years. And this change just happens to have coincided with the period, beginning around 1987, when higher education came under intense public criticism for radicalism and elitism—the period of the "culture wars."[24]

There are several reasons why more women and non-white Americans, not to mention more non-Americans, began

[21] Martin J. Finkelstein, Robert K. Seal, and Jack H. Schuster, *The New Academic Generation: A Profession in Transformation* (Baltimore: Johns Hopkins University Press, 1998), pp. 26–32.

[22] *Part-Time, Adjunct, and Temporary Faculty: The New Majority?: Report of the Sloan Conference on Part-Time and Adjunct Faculty* ([New York]: Alfred P. Sloan Foundation, 1998), p. 5.

[23] Doctor's degrees conferred by institutions of higher education, by racial/ethnic group and sex of student: 1976–77 to 1996–97, *Digest of Education Statistics*.

[24] The "culture wars" encompassed more than higher education. A main target of criticism, starting in 1989, was the funding practices of the National Endowments for the Arts and the Humanities. See Richard Bolton, ed., *Culture Wars: Documents from the Recent Controversies in the Arts* (New York: New Press, 1992).

entering higher education in greater proportions after 1970, but one of them is simply structural. After 1970, there were fewer white American males for colleges to choose from. In order to maintain enrollments and selectivity, colleges simply had to enlarge the pool from which they accepted new students. The system had overexpanded during the Golden Age. In 1950, there were 2.6 million college students; in 1970, there were 8 million. Too many state-subsidized slots had been created—in 1950, 50 percent of college students attended a public institution; in 1970, 73 percent did—and the result was a much higher level of competition for new students.[25] There had been talk before 1975 about the educational desirability of co-educational and mixed-race student bodies, but at many schools, economic necessity is what made it happen. That is a reason why after 1970, virtually every non-military all-male college in the United States went co-ed. It was not the women's movement that did it. Or, more precisely, the same need for a stronger labor force pool that enabled the movement for equal rights for women finally to have some success applied to higher education as well.[26]

The intellectual changes in many of the academic disciplines, and particularly in the humanities, have the same etiology. This does not mean that changes in the humanities disciplines were triggered by changes in demographics,

[25] Lazerson, "The Disappointments of Success," p. 66.

[26] The argument about economic necessity is the conclusion of Duffy and Goldberg's *Crafting a Class*, a study of admissions policy at sixteen Ohio and Massachusetts liberal arts colleges. On the women's movement and the rise of the information economy, see Francis Fukuyama, *The Great Disruption: Human Nature and the Reconstitution of Social Order* (New York: The Free Press, 1999).

although this has often been asserted. It means that the factors that contributed to the new demographic makeup of higher education are the same as those that contributed to the present condition of the humanities disciplines. The two phenomena are both fallout from the Golden Age.

3.

The strategic rationale for the postwar expansion in American higher education was technological and geopolitical— we needed better hardware than the Communists—but the social policy rationale was meritocratic. Postwar educational leaders, including James Conant and George Zook, were concerned about broadening the range of educational opportunity for all Americans,[27] and, as we have seen, the National Defense Education Act was quite explicit on this point. If the nation seeks to maximize its talent pool in the name of greater national security or greater economic productivity or both, it will not wish to limit entrants to that pool on the basis of considerations extraneous to aptitude, such as gender, family income, and skin color. Postwar liberals like Conant also believed that inherited privilege leads to class resentments, and that class resentments lead to conditions in which illiberal political movements can grow.

The meritocratic philosophy was accompanied by two other postwar developments. One was a belief in the importance of general education in undergraduate teaching; the other was

[27] See *General Education in a Free Society: Report of the Harvard Committee* (Cambridge, MA: Harvard University Press, 1945), and *Higher Education for American Democracy: A Report of the President's Commission on Higher Education* (New York: Harper & Bros., 1948).

the dominance of a scientific model in academic research. In practice, most colleges paid lip service to general education in American universities after the war; relatively few created independent general education curricula.[28] But such curricula were not necessary for the idea to have an effect, since general education did receive a great deal of lip service. Most educators subscribed to the belief that the major works of the Western tradition are accessible to all students in more or less the same way; that those works constitute a more or less coherent body of thought (or, at least, a coherent debate); and that they can serve as a kind of benign cultural ideology in a pluralist nation whose citizens are generally wary of anything overtly ideological.

The other critical Golden Age development, the adoption of a self-consciously scientific model of research, also reflected the anti-ideological temper of postwar American thought, a temper epitomized in the phrase, first used in the conferences of the anti-Communist Congress for Cultural Freedom and later given wider circulation by the sociologist Daniel Bell, "the end of ideology."[29] To some extent the antipathy to ideology was a response to global political history between 1914 and 1945. But to some extent, as the historian Thomas Bender has suggested, it was a response to all that federal money that began pouring into universities after the war. Scholars eschewed political implications in their research because they wished not to offend their grant-

---

[28] As we saw in chapter one.

[29] Daniel Bell, *The End of Ideology: On the Exhaustion of Political Ideas in the Fifties* (New York: The Free Press, 1962). The phrase is also associated with the sociologist Seymour Martin Lipset.

ing agencies.[30] The idea that academics, particularly in the social sciences, could provide the state with neutral research results on which pragmatic public policies could be based was an animating idea in the 1950s university. In the sciences, it helped establish what the Harvard sociologist Talcott Parsons called the ethos of "cognitive rationality."[31] In the study of political history, it led to the "consensus approach," an attempt to avoid distracting ideological debate when writing and teaching history. In sociology, it produced what Robert Merton, the Columbia sociologist, called "theories of the middle range," which emphasized the formulation of limited hypotheses subject to empirical verification.[32] Behaviorism and rational choice theory became dominant paradigms in psychology and political science. In literature, even when the temperament was anti-positivistic, as in the case of the New Criticism and structuralism, the methods were scientistic.[33]

[30] Thomas Bender, "Politics, Intellect, and the American University, 1945–1995," in Bender and Carl E. Schorske, eds., *American Academic Culture in Transformation: Fifty Years, Four Disciplines* (Princeton: Princeton University Press, 1997), pp. 17–54. In the early Cold War period, of course, the tendency to avoid the political was also a response to the threat of McCarthyite intrusions into the academic process. See Ellen W. Shrecker, *No Ivory Tower: McCarthyism and the Universities* (New York: Oxford University Press, 1986).

[31] Talcott Parsons and Gerald M. Platt, *The American University* (Cambridge, MA: Harvard University Press, 1973), p. 47, and Geiger, *Research and Relevant Knowledge*, pp. 331–32.

[32] Robert K. Merton, *Social Theory and Social Structure*, rev. ed. (New York: The Free Press, 1968), pp. 39–72. The first edition of Merton's book was published in 1949.

[33] See Wallace Martin, "Criticism and the Academy," in A. Walton Litz, Louis Menand, and Lawrence Rainey, eds., *The Cambridge History of Literary Criticism*. Vol. 7: *Modernism and the New Criticism* (Cambridge: Cambridge University Press, 2000), pp. 269–321.

Boundaries were respected and methodologies were codified. Discipline reigned in the disciplines. Scholars in the fifties who looked back on their prewar educations tended to be appalled by what they now regarded as a lack of analytic rigor and focus.[34]

Because public money was being pumped into the system at the high end—into the large research universities—the effect of the Golden Age was to make the research professor the type of the professor generally. This is a phenomenon that the sociologists Christopher Jencks and David Riesman tracked in their study of what they called "the academic revolution"—the emergence of higher education as a central source of social authority.[35] For the first time in the history of American higher education, research, rather than teaching or service, defined the model for the professor—not only in the doctoral institutions, but all the way down the institutional ladder. This strengthened the grip of the disciplines on scholarly and pedagogical practice. Professors identified with their disciplines, which constitute a national "community," first and with their institutions second. Federal research grants increased by a factor of four between 1960 and 1990, but faculty teaching hours decreased by half, from nine hours a week to four and a half.[36] Few professors would have said

[34] See the essays in Bender and Schorske, eds., *American Academic Culture in Transformation*, esp. Carl E. Schorske, "The New Rigorism in the Human Sciences, 1940–1960," pp. 309–29.

[35] On the trend "from localism to nationalism," see Christopher Jencks and David Riesman, *The Academic Revolution* (Garden City, NY: Doubleday, 1968), pp. 155–98.

[36] Clark Kerr, *The Uses of the University*, 4th ed. (Cambridge, MA: Harvard University Press, 1995), pp. 83, 142.

that their jobs became easier because they were teaching less; the demand for research simply was much greater. This is how it was that the system of higher education became more uniform even as it expanded between 1945 and 1975. The Cold War homogenized the academic profession.

It now seems obvious that the dispensation put into place in the first two decades of the Cold War was just waiting for the tiniest spark to blow sky-high. And the spark, when it came, wasn't so tiny. The war in Vietnam exposed almost every weakness in the system that Conant and his generation of educational leaders had constructed, from the dangers inherent in the university's financial dependence on the state to the way its social role was figured in national security policy to the degree of factitiousness in the value-neutral standard of research in fields outside the natural sciences. (The war did also lead to skepticism about the neutrality of academic science, though this criticism was political as well as philosophical.)

Then, after 1970, as new populations began to arrive in numbers in American universities, the meritocratic rationale was exploded as well. For it turned out that cultural differences were not only not so easy to bracket as men like Conant had imagined; those differences suddenly began to seem a lot more interesting than the similarities. The trend was made irreversible by Justice Lewis Powell's decision in *Regents of the University of California v. Bakke*, handed down in 1978.[37] That case was brought by a white man, Allan Bakke, who had twice been rejected for admission to the medical school at the University of California at Davis, even though his scores were

---

[37] *Regents of the University of California v. Bakke*, 438 U.S. 265.

higher than those of non-white applicants who did receive offers of admission. The U.S. Supreme Court upheld the decision of the California State Supreme Court, and ruled, by a 5–4 vote, that Bakke had been denied his rights under the Equal Protection clause. But, by the back door, it also gave the consideration of race in admissions constitutional sanction.

Justice Powell's decision, quoting from the *amici curiae* brief filed jointly for Columbia, Harvard, Stanford, and the University of Pennsylvania, pointed out that college admissions offices have always given preference to various types of candidates whose grades and standardized test scores may be below the average. They have done so because they have other institutional needs besides putting scholars in the classrooms. They have football teams to field, orchestras and marching bands to staff, student organizations to be led, alumni to be kept in a giving mood, and feeder schools to be kept in a feeding mood. They have a gender balance to preserve. They can't have ten times as many poets as physicists, or thirty students from Exeter and none from the local high school. Racial diversity, Powell concluded, is just another institutional need. What the *Bakke* decision basically said to universities was: Stop talking about quotas and about redressing the effects of past discrimination and start talking about the educational benefits of mixed-race student bodies, and you'll be on the safe side of the law. It preserved the practice by changing the rationale.

Powell's opinion changed the language of college admissions. He blew a hole in meritocratic theory, because he stated what might have been obvious to anyone looking for it from the beginning, which is that college admissions, even and especially at places like Harvard, have never been purely meritocratic. Colleges have always taken non-standardized and non-standardizable attributes into account when selecting students, from musical prodigies to football stars, alumni legacies, and the offspring of local bigwigs. If a college admitted only students who got top scores on the SATs, it would have a very boring class. "Diversity" is the very word that Powell used in the *Bakke* opinion, and there are probably few college Web sites in the United States today in which the word "diversity," or one of its cognates, does not appear.

The term plainly connotes racial diversity. College admissions officers sometimes use the phrase "three in a tree." It is a reference to the now-standard admissions brochure photograph of three college students on or around a tree— each identifiably a member of a different racial group. But "diversity" also means a variety of interests and abilities. Colleges no longer search for (in admissions office shorthand) BWRKs—bright well-rounded kids. They search for what they call "well-lopsided" applicants. They no longer want well-rounded students; they want a well-rounded class.[38]

4.

As the homogeneity of the student body broke down after 1975, and the homogeneity of the faculty broke down along with it, the humanities disciplines underwent a series of

---

[38] A good journalistic account of contemporary admissions practices (at Wesleyan) is Jacques Steinberg, *The Gatekeepers: Inside the Admissions Process of a Premier College* (New York: Viking, 2002). See also, for a look at one of the methods some elite colleges use to achieve a diverse class, Christopher Avery, Andrew Fairbanks, and Richard Zeckhauser, *The Early Admissions Game: Joining the Elite* (Cambridge, MA: Harvard University Press, 2003).

transformations. These shifts became visible at the level of the undergraduate curriculum in an emphasis on multicultural-ism (meaning exposure to specifically ethnic perspectives and traditions) and values (attention to the ethical implications of knowledge); in a renewed interest in service (manifested in the emergence of internship and off-campus social service programs) and the idea of community; in "education for citi-zenship"; and in a revival of a conception of teaching, asso-ciated with the philosopher John Dewey, as a collaborative process of learning and inquiry. The landmark study identify-ing this shift is *Scholarship Reconsidered*, by Ernest Boyer, the president of the Carnegie Foundation for the Advancement of Teaching, which was published in 1990.[39]

This transformation in the undergraduate curriculum was clearly a reaction against the model created by the Golden Age and the academic revolution: the model of disinterested research and the great books or "Western Civ" curriculum. The vocabulary of "disinterestedness," "objectivity," "reason," and "knowledge," and talk about things like "the scientific method," "the canon," and "the fact/value distinction" began to be superseded, particularly in the humanities, by attention to "interpretations" (rather than "facts"), "perspective" (rather than "objectivity"), and "understanding" (rather than "reason" or "analysis"). An emphasis on universalism and "greatness" was replaced by an emphasis on diversity and difference; the scientistic norms that once prevailed in many of the "soft"

---

[39] Ernest L. Boyer, *Scholarship Reconsidered: Priorities of the Professoriate* (San Francisco: Carnegie Foundation for the Advancement of Teaching, 1990). See also Bruce Kimball, *The Condition of American Liberal Education: Pragmatism and a Changing Tradition* (New York: College Entrance Examinations Board, 1995), a study largely confirming Boyer's conclusions.

disciplines began to be viewed with skepticism (though a very *rigorous* skepticism); context and contingency were continually appealed to; attention to "objects" gave way to attention to "representations." The area in which these transformations were most emphatic was literature, especially English and French, the fields in which much of the theorizing took place. The influence of that theorizing spread across the humanities disciplines and, during the seventies and eighties, extended into history departments, anthropology departments, and even law schools.

This trend was fundamentally a backlash against the excessive respect for disciplinarity of the Golden Age university. The trend should not be attributed to demographic diversification, because its first theorists were mostly white men, and because the seeds of the undoing of the old disciplinary models were already present within the models themselves. The artificiality of Golden Age disciplinarity made an implosion inevitable. Fields of inquiry become formalized and institutionalized by drawing borders that differentiate them from other fields. The university is, in this sense, a semiotic system: a discipline defines itself in relation to all the disciplines it is not. The study of literature is not the study of philosophy or sociology or history; it stands on its own intellectual foundation. But the more rigidly a discipline's borders are enforced and the more autonomy it claims, the more vulnerable it is to subversion. Either the premises on which the discipline rests can be extended *ad absurdum*, or it can be shown that the discipline is suppressing some relevant aspect of its subject matter (and this suppressed aspect usually turns out, in the new dispensation, to be what was secretly driving everything else all along).

Take the example of English departments. To the extent that, in the fifties and sixties, teaching and writing in literary studies relied on the notion that texts can be interpreted noncontextually, as stand-alone verbal artifacts, and that these interpretations have hard-and-fast degrees of validity—in other words, that the close reading of literary texts is all by itself a discipline whose practices are transmissible and whose results are verifiable—those departments were exposed to two species of anti-disciplinary virus. One involved pushing the possibilities of interpretation "into the abyss," as deconstructionists put it—showing that there is no place for interpretation to end, no place for the interpreter to say "This is the limit of what the text can mean," and that there is nothing outside the process of interpretation against which to measure an interpretation's validity. The other virus was the political. Of course works of literature are embedded in systems of representation that reflect, and play some role in the perpetuation of, the political structures of their times. In the 1970s, it suddenly became important, just as a consequence of the ordinary process of inquiry, to say this and to explore the implications. Poststructuralism and cultural studies were not alien invasions in literary studies. They grew out of the normal practices of literature professors.

And this is true of the work of virtually all the influential figures in the sixties and seventies who are associated with the transformation of scholarly approaches from formalist and universalist to historicist and hermeneutical. Thomas Kuhn (history of science), Paul de Man (French and comparative literature), Hayden White (history), Clifford Geertz (anthropology), Richard Rorty (philosophy), and Stanley Fish

(English):[40] it is not a group of people that any contemporary college catalogue would feel comfortable calling "diverse." They were all white males and their work took place entirely within the disciplinary frameworks in which they had been trained. De Man's criticism, which played a major role in introducing deconstruction to American academics, was in many respects the culmination of the New Critical tradition of close rhetorical analysis, just as Fish's was the culmination of the reader-response approach pioneered by two of the founders of modern English studies, I. A. Richards and William Empson.[41] Clifford Geertz's influential book proposing what he called a semiotic theory of culture grew out of one of the most straightforward acts of discipline making in the Cold War period, Talcott Parsons's division of the social sciences into three spheres: the social system (the province of sociology); the personality system (psychology); and the cultural system (anthropology).[42] *Philosophy and the Mirror of Nature,*

---

[40] Thomas Kuhn, *The Structure of Scientific Revolutions* (1962; 2nd ed., Chicago: University of Chicago Press, 1970); Paul de Man, *Blindness and Insight: Essays in the Rhetoric of Contemporary Criticism* (New York: Oxford University Press, 1971); Hayden White, *Metahistory: The Historical Imagination in Nineteenth-Century Europe* (Baltimore: Johns Hopkins University Press, 1973); Clifford Geertz, *The Interpretation of Cultures* (New York: Basic Books, 1973); Richard Rorty, *Philosophy and the Mirror of Nature* (Princeton: Princeton University Press, 1979); and Stanley Fish, *Is There a Text in This Class? The Authority of Interpretive Communities* (Cambridge, MA: Harvard University Press, 1980).

[41] I. A. Richards, *Practical Criticism: A Study of Literary Judgment* (New York: Harcourt, Brace, 1929); William Empson, *Seven Types of Ambiguity* (London: Chatto & Windus, 1930).

[42] Talcott Parsons, *The Social System* (Glencoe, IL: The Free Press, 1951). Parsons, who founded the interdisciplinary Department of Social Relations at Harvard, intended the three disciplines to complement and interact with one another.

Rorty's attempt to put an end to, or to transcend, the analytic tradition in philosophy, constructs its argument entirely from within the tradition of analytic philosophy, just as *The Structure of Scientific Revolutions*, Kuhn's revisionist interpretation of the history of science, is a perfectly conventional work in the philosophy and history of science. None of these scholars was attacking his discipline from the outside.

Nor were they making explicitly political critiques. Kuhn's book is emphatically not a work of science studies. But science studies—inquiry into the social and political context of scientific research—is what it helped to bring about. And there is no question that this turn in the intellectual dialectic fed into the collapse of the race- and gender-blind ideal of meritocratic educational theory. It gave members of groups previously excluded from or marginalized within the academy equipment for the business of criticizing the limitations of Cold War–era disciplines. When the politically consequential critiques *did* arrive—for example, in literary studies, via work associated with scholars such as Edward Said (postcolonial studies), Sandra Gilbert and Susan Gubar (feminist criticism), Eve Kosofsky Sedgwick (queer theory), and Fredric Jameson (Marxist criticism)—an alternative critical paradigm was already in place.[43]

---

[43] Edward Said, *Orientalism* (New York: Pantheon, 1978); Sandra Gilbert and Susan Gubar, *The Madwoman in the Attic: The Woman Writer and the Nineteenth-Century Literary Imagination* (New Haven: Yale University Press, 1979); Fredric Jameson, *The Political Unconscious: Narrative as a Socially Symbolic Act* (Ithaca, NY: Cornell University Press, 1981); and Eve Kosofsky Sedgwick, *Between Men: English Literature and Male Homosocial Desire* (New York: Columbia University Press, 1985). And see the essays in Henry Louis Gates, Jr., ed., *"Race," Writing, and Difference* (Chicago: University of Chicago Press, 1986). The list is somewhat arbitrary, but it indicates roughly the timing and

5.

The revolution in the humanities disciplines happened in two stages. In the beginning, what took place was not a redefinition of disciplinarity; it was a kind of anti-disciplinarity. Academic activity (peer-reviewed publications, dissertations, and some teaching) began flowing toward paradigms that defined themselves essentially in antagonism toward traditional disciplines. These new paradigms justified themselves as means of accommodating what the old paradigms were leaving out. Women's studies, cultural studies, science studies, gay and lesbian studies, postcolonial studies, and so on are all non-departmental by bureaucratic design—that is, they generally do not have their own faculty lines or award terminal degrees (sometimes they are allowed to award "certificates")—and they are interdisciplinary by definition. Faculty members in women's studies came from a variety of disciplines, from literature and sociology to the natural sciences. The standard institutional niche for these activities was the center.

Anti-disciplinarity arose from the marriage of the theoretical position that the disciplines are limiting and factitious ways to organize knowledge with the institutional failure, initially, to integrate new areas of inquiry adequately into the traditional departments. The fundamental rationale for women's studies was the perception of a gender bias in the disciplines: that is why its spirit was, in the beginning, fundamentally anti-disciplinary. The centers came into being because the

---

shape of this moment in the history of literary studies. A detailed account can be found in Christa Knellwolf and Christopher Norris, eds., *The Cambridge History of Literary Criticism*. Vol. 9: *Twentieth-Century Historical, Philosophical, and Psychological Perspectives* (Cambridge: Cambridge University Press, 2001).

traditional departments, staffed largely by Golden Agers, did not recognize gender or ethnic identity as valid rubrics for teaching or scholarship. Outside the discipline became the good place to be, and there was a period in the eighties and nineties when some disciplines were almost defined by the internal critiques they generated. The stars were the people who talked about the failures and omissions in their own fields.

When it became clear, in those years, that a split was developing between Golden Age and post–Golden Age approaches to inquiry, it was common to argue for a teach-the-conflicts resolution, an idea championed notably by the English professor Gerald Graff.[44] The notion was that professors might neutralize the divisiveness within their own disciplines by making that divisiveness the subject of their teaching. But this teach-the-conflicts approach eventually came to seem otiose because resistance to the new paradigms largely evaporated (or took early retirement). New courses were added to department offerings: in 1997, the *New York Times* reported that courses on sexual identity could be found in virtually every liberal arts college catalogue in the country.[45] The traditionalists were co-opted. And so, in a way, were the iconoclasts. They awakened to find that history, in its cun-

---

[44] Gerald Graff, *Beyond the Culture Wars: How Teaching the Conflicts Can Revitalize American Education* (New York: W. W. Norton, 1992). See also Francis Oakley, *Community of Learning: The American College and the Liberal Arts Tradition* (New York: Oxford University Press, 1992), pp. 160–64. Oakley has an interdisciplinary dialogue in mind; Graff's is essentially intradisciplinary.

[45] Ethan Bronner, "Study of Sex Experiencing 2d Revolution," *New York Times,* December 28, 1997.

ning, has made them rulers of the towns they once set out to burn down.

What took place after the nineties was not exactly a return to disciplinarity. It was a movement in two only partly related directions: toward interdisciplinarity, and toward what might be called postdisciplinarity. These terms are harder to define than they seem. What true interdisciplinarity might look like no one really knows.[46] Postdisciplinarity signifies a variety of tendencies, including methodological eclecticism, boundary-crossing work (a literature professor writing on music or fashion), post-professionalism (writing for a non-academic audience), and the role of the public intellectual. These trends were not consistent across the disciplines, though. Some fields were transformed and some were not. Anthropology became more postdisciplinary; sociology did not. English became highly interdisciplinary; comparative literature, a field that has always been definitionally challenged, sought a heightened sense of disciplinarity. History, for the most part, was accommodating to the new dispensation. Social history and other "ground-up" approaches were added to traditional approaches, and historians engaged with the problematics of objectivity and interpretation. Philosophy, on the other hand, was not so accommodating. Rorty was persona non grata in the philosophy departments at the two universities where he worked in the second half of his career, the University of Virginia and Stanford. At Stanford, his appointment was in Comparative Literature. One of the reasons Jacques Derrida is persistently identified as a literary critic in the United States

---

[46] Some of the problems with interdisciplinarity are discussed in chapter three.

(he was a philosopher) is because when he taught in American universities he was a guest of literature departments. His work, like the work of many European philosophers who are associated with structuralist and poststructuralist thought, remains virtually untaught in American philosophy departments. The existence of incompatible scholarly standards and assumptions across the different liberal arts fields is part of the problem people searching for a consensus paradigm for humanities scholarship face.

The unevenness turns up quickly in any comparative look at undergraduate curricula. The biggest change in college catalogues after 1970 was an enormous increase in the number of offerings, even in departments in which enrollments remained constant.[47] At the same time, courses became much more specialized; that is, the broad survey or introductory course began to disappear, something that is usually a symptom of uncertainty about the essential character of a discipline. But the changes are interestingly uneven, as though some colleges and departments make a point of clinging to a narrow definition that other colleges and departments make a point of rejecting. In the catalogue for Trinity College, for example, the philosophy department's announcement asserts: "A good philosopher should know at least a little something about everything." The department then recommends the study of a foreign language, but only because it "encourages the habit of careful attention to a text." It recommends a "broad understanding of modern science," but suggests that

---

[47] Francis Oakley, "Ignorant Armies and Nighttime Clashes: Changes in the Humanities Classroom, 1970–1995," in Kernan, ed., *What's Happened to the Humanities?*, pp. 63–83.

"any good science course . . . is suitable." It goes on to recommend courses in history, literature, and the arts, but advises that students generally select courses in these fields according to the amount of reading assigned (the more reading, the more desirable). It ends by saying what was already clear enough: "We require no particular nondepartmental courses as part of the major." The next section, entitled "Introductory Courses," begins: "There is no single best way to be introduced to philosophy."[48] At Carleton, on the other hand, philosophy majors are required to take one of three introductory courses; courses in logic, metaphysics, epistemology, and ethics; and a course in the history of philosophy, as well as electives and advanced courses.[49]

To take another example, compare the English departments at two otherwise quite similar schools, Amherst and Wellesley.[50] English majors at Wellesley are required to take ten English department courses, eight of which must be in literature. (Wellesley's English department also offers a number of courses in film.) Basic writing courses do not count toward the major. All English majors must take a core course called "Critical Interpretation"; one course on Shakespeare; and at least two courses on literature written before 1900, one of which must be on literature written before 1800. Cross-

---

[48] http://www.trincoll.edu/depts/phil/major.html. Material from college Web sites is always subject to change, of course. It might seem as though Trinity's description is only a Socratic definition of philosophy as open-ended inquiry, and perfectly traditional. I was told by a member of the Trinity department, though, that it was, in fact, designed to avoid the suggestion that philosophy is an autonomous discipline.

[49] http://apps.carleton.edu/curricular/philosophy/major/.

[50] http://www.amherst.edu/~english/; http://www.wellesley.edu/English/.

listed courses—that is, interdisciplinary courses—are, with
one exception, not counted toward the major. The course list-
ing reflects attention to every traditional historical period
in English and American literature. Down the turnpike at
Amherst, on the other hand, English majors have only to
take ten courses "offered or approved by the department"—in
other words, apparently, they may be courses in any department. Majors have no core requirement and no period requirements. They must simply take one lower- and one upper-level
course, and they must declare, during their senior year, a "concentration," consisting of three courses whose relatedness they
must argue to the department. The catalogue assures students
that "the choices of courses and description of the area of
concentration may be revised as late as the end of the add-
drop period of a student's last semester." Course listings, as
they appear online, are not historically comprehensive, and
many upper-level offerings focus on such topics as African
(not African-American) writers. At Amherst, in short, the
English department has a highly permissive attitude toward
its majors. At Wellesley, the department evidently holds an
opposing view, envisioning the field more substantively and
concretely. What this contrast suggests is that there has been
a great deal of paradigm loss within the humanities disciplines, and that this loss is manifesting itself at the undergraduate level, as well.

What the recent history of the disciplines does suggest,
though, is that it is wise to avoid the following narrative:
when more women and non-whites came into the system,
traditional norms of scholarly constraint disappeared. The
argument is not that this narrative is undesirable—although,
amazingly, one sometimes hears proponents of diversity reit-

erating an upbeat version of it. The argument is that the narrative is incorrect. Within the history of higher education, the Cold War university was the anomaly, and what are criticized as deviations and diffusions in the present system are largely reactions against that earlier dispensation. People may admire the old dispensation, or feel some nostalgia for it, but it was fundamentally untenable.

6.

What the humanities experienced between 1970 and 1990 was the intellectual and institutional equivalent of a revolution. Despite what some critics claimed, the humanities did not make themselves irrelevant by this transformation. On the contrary: the humanities helped to make the rest of the academic world alive to issues surrounding objectivity and interpretation, and to the significance of racial and gender difference. Scholars in the humanities were complicating social science models of human motivation and behavior for years before social scientists began doing the same thing via research in cognitive science. That political and economic behavior is often non-rational is not news to literature professors. And humanists can hope that someday more social scientists and psychologists will consider the mediating role of culture in their accounts of belief and behavior.

But do fields such as literature, philosophy, and the arts need to have consistent, stable, and articulable paradigms for research and teaching? Paradigms are put into place by including some methods and subject matter and excluding other methods and subject matter, and this means that, informally, paradigm creation and paradigm enforcement are always going on. Trying to avoid them is like giving every student an A: not everything can count, and part of the purpose of organized knowledge production is deciding what does count and what does not. But how formal do these paradigms need to be?

Most of the shocks to the philosophical foundations of teaching and scholarship in the humanities, from the interpretive turn in the sixties and seventies to the diversity turn in the eighties and nineties, arose from challenges to prevailing understandings of what counts. Legitimacy—is this really knowledge or is it something else?—was precisely what was at stake in that revolution.[51] It is probably impossible, after the revolution, to put the toothpaste back in the tube. Eclecticism seems to be the fate of the academic humanities. But there is no reason why that cannot in itself constitute a claim to legitimacy. If one part of the university is (along with its many other projects) continually enacting a "crisis of institutional legitimation," it is performing a service for the rest of the university. It is pursuing an ongoing inquiry into the limits of inquiry. And it is not just asking questions about knowledge; it is creating knowledge by asking the questions. Skepticism about the forms of knowledge is itself a form of knowledge.

---

[51] Humanities professors coined a number of clever phrases for the "crisis of legitimation." My favorite is the title of an MLA paper by David H. Richter: "Once I Built a Railroad, Now It's Done. Buddy, Can You Paradigm?"

3

Interdisciplinarity
and Anxiety

1.

THERE ARE FEW TERMS in twenty-first-century higher education with a greater buzz factor than "interdisciplinarity"—the name for teaching and scholarship that bring together methods and materials from more than one academic discipline. No one, or almost no one, says a word against it. It is evoked by professors and by deans with equal enthusiasm. And in some fields, job and fellowship applicants find it almost de rigueur to stress the interdisciplinarity of their research. The buzziness has to do with the suggestion that interdisciplinarity is a new way to organize teaching and scholarship, that it holds out the promise of some kind of unification of knowledge (scientists and humanists speaking the same language, for example), and even that it is mildly transgressive—that it can refresh old paradigms and, almost by itself, generate radically new perspectives and ideas, that it can put scholarship into closer touch with life. Interdisciplinarity stands for the notion that what is holding things back is disciplinarity, the persistence of the academic silos known as departments, and that if colleges and universities could get past that outmoded dispensation, a lot of their problems would disappear.

With all these possibilities hovering over it, talk about interdisciplinarity tends to have an anxious tone. But it is hard to see how interdisciplinarity is an adequate correlative to the anxiety. The anxiety feels existential, and interdisciplinarity is, at bottom, a professional and institutional issue. Interdisciplinarity is attainable to the extent that professors are professionally motivated and institutionally supported to practice it. Professors may not be so motivated and institutions may not be supportive. But interdisciplinarity is not, as a thing in itself, subversive or transgressive or transformational or even new.[1] In many respects, interdisciplinarity is a ratification of existing arrangements. And it can become a rationale for future arrangements that are less accommodating than the ones professors live with now. So what are academics talking about when they talk about interdisciplinarity? Is it really interdisciplinarity? Do they care about interdisciplinarity *as such*? Or is there something else that they are anxious about for which talk of interdisciplinarity serves as a kind of screen discourse?

One reason to suspect that interdisciplinarity is not what people are really talking about when they talk about interdisciplinarity is that when you ask them why interdisciplinarity is important, they often answer by saying that it solves the problem of disciplinarity. But this is a non sequitur. Interdisciplinarity is simply disciplinarity raised to a higher power. It is not an escape from disciplinarity; it is the scholarly and

---

[1] A point made, and more than once, by Stanley Fish: see Fish, "Being Interdisciplinary Is So Very Hard to Do," *There's No Such Thing as Free Speech and It's a Good Thing, Too* (New York: Oxford University Press, 1994), pp. 213–42, and *Professional Correctness: Literary Studies and Political Change* (Cambridge, MA: Harvard University Press, 1995), pp. 71–92.

pedagogical ratification of disciplinarity. If it is disciplinarity that academics want to get rid of, then they cannot call the new order interdisciplinarity. They also cannot call the new order anti-disciplinarity. It might be called postdisciplinarity, but that is asking for trouble. Maybe academics are stuck. Being stuck can certainly be a reason for anxiety. How did higher education get to a place where interdisciplinarity became a vision of salvation?

2.

The place to begin talking about interdisciplinarity is disciplinarity, and the first (and obvious) thing to be said about disciplinarity is that the disciplines are not what philosophers call natural kinds. The academic disciplines do not carve knowledge at the joints, and they did not drop down out of God's blue sky. The disciplines were constructed at a particular historical moment, and teachers and students in the twenty-first-century university are the heirs of that moment. Understanding how and for what purposes that construction was accomplished gives us a little bit of help in understanding why disciplinarity is so firmly rooted in educational practice that academics can name an alternative to it interdisciplinarity.

Academic disciplinarity—the creation and institutionalization of separate and effectively autonomous departments of research—is an episode in the history of the division of labor. The disciplines emerged with the modern research university, between 1870 and 1915. That period, only forty-five years, was the big bang of American higher education. It saw the creation of new institutions and the conversion of existing ones to the model we know today: a program of undergraduate instruction joined to a graduate and professional school operation designed for training researchers and producing specialized research. Almost every aspect of higher education that we are familiar with dates from this period: undergraduate electives; the requirement of a bachelor's degree for admission to professional school; graduate schools for the education of specialists who will educate the undergraduates; the expectation that faculty will have doctorates and produce scholarly publications; and the articulation of the principle of academic freedom, signaled by the founding of the American Association of University Professors in 1915. And two other developments, as well: the establishment of national professional associations for scholars and the creation of the modern academic departments.

As the historian Walter Metzger says, "Between 1870 and 1900 nearly every subject in the academic curriculum was fitted out with a new or refurbished external organization—a learned or disciplinary association, national in membership and specialized in scope—and with a new and modified internal organization—a department of instruction made the building block of most academic administrations. These were more than formal arrangements of the campus workforce; they testified to and tightened the hold of specialization in academic life."[2] We can see the creation of the "new

2 Walter Metzger, "The Academic Profession in the United States," in Burton R. Clark, ed., *The Academic Profession: National, Disciplinary, and Institutional Settings* (Berkeley: University of California Press, 1987), p. 136. See also Andrew Abbott, *Chaos of Disciplines* (Chicago: University of Chicago Press, 2001), pp. 122–23: "The departmental structure of the American university has remained largely unchanged since its creation between 1890 and 1910. Biology, it is true, has fractured in most universities into a number of departments. . . . In the humanities and social science, the departmental map has shown only

or refurbished external organization" Metzger mentions in the evolution of the American Social Science Association (ASSA), which was founded in 1865 as a group for amateur students in a broadly defined range of social science subjects. After 1880, the ASSA split up, rather rapidly, into separate groups of modern language teachers and scholars, the Modern Language Association (founded in 1883); the American Historical Association (founded in 1884); and associations for economists (1885), church historians (1888), folklorists (1888), and political scientists (1889). The American Mathematical Society was formed in 1888, the American Physical Society in 1889, and the American Sociological Society in 1905—all university-based communities of academic professionals, jealous of the autonomy of their disciplines and (as is still the case) with no umbrella organization coordinating their intellectual activities.[3]

At the same time that these national scholarly associations were establishing themselves, universities were undergoing an equally rapid period of department formation, and by 1900 a departmental system of administration was in place in most of the leading schools. In other words, academic work was completely restructured inside the span of a single genera-

---

marginal changes in the last sixty or eighty years. Linguistics, comparative literature, and a few other small fields are the only and occasional newcomers."

[3] There are national scholarly and scientific organizations, such as the American Council of Learned Societies (ACLS), which was founded in 1919 and which provides a common organizational home for humanities and related social science disciplines. But most professors do not gather regularly in these venues, and their purpose is not to transcend disciplinarity.

tion.[4] And the restructuring accompanied a dramatic expansion of the system. In 1870, there were 563 institutions of higher learning in the United States with 63,000 students. By 1900, there were 977 institutions and 238,000 students. In 1930, there were 1,409 schools enrolling 1.1 million students. There were 5,553 professors in the United States in 1870; in 1890, there were 15,809; in 1930, there were 23,868.[5]

The rise of the modern university and the emergence of the modern academic disciplines were part of the same phenomenon: the professionalization of occupation.[6] Professionaliza-

[4] On the evolution of specific disciplines, see Gerald Graff, *Professing Literature: An Institutional History* (Chicago: University of Chicago Press, 1987); Thomas L. Haskell, *The Emergence of Professional Social Science: The American Social Science Association and the Nineteenth-Century Crisis of Authority* (Urbana: University of Illinois Press, 1977); Bruce Kuklick, *The Rise of American Philosophy: Cambridge, Massachusetts, 1860–1930* (New Haven: Yale University Press, 1977); and Bruce Mazlish, *A New Science: The Breakdown of Connections and the Birth of Sociology* (New York: Oxford University Press, 1989).

[5] Enrollment in institutions of higher education, by sex, enrollment status, and type of institution: 1869–1995; Institutions of higher education—colleges and universities, teacher-training institutions, and medical and dental schools, by public-private control: 1869–1995; and Professional and instructional staff at institutions of higher education, by sex and public-private control: 1869–1993, *Historical Statistics of the United States: Millennial Edition online*, at http://hsus.cambridge.org.

[6] On the sociology of professionalism, see Magali Sarfatti Larson, *The Rise of Professionalism: A Sociological Analysis* (Berkeley: University of California Press, 1977). On the history of professionalism, particularly as it relates to higher education, see Burton J. Bledstein, *The Culture of Professionalism: The Middle Class and the Development of Higher Education in America* (New York: W. W. Norton, 1976), and Bruce Kimball, *The "True Professional Ideal" in America: A History* (Lanham, MD: Rowman and Littlefield, 1995). I discuss professionalism and literary modernism in *Discovering Modernism: T. S. Eliot and His Context* (New York: Oxford University Press, 1987), pp. 97–132. Some of what follows is adapted from those pages.

tion means two things: credentialization and specialization. A professional is a person who is licensed—by earning a degree, taking an examination, or passing some other qualifying test—to practice in a specialized field. The late nineteenth century was a period of rapidly increasing professionalization; in fact, one of the reasons higher education transformed itself after 1870 was so that it could operate as the main social institution for training professionals. Universities are very good at this. They have requirements for entrance and requirements for exit, so they make an efficient, standardized, and highly visible gateway. The period that saw the creation of the academic disciplines and their national associations was also the period that saw the professionalization of occupations such as medicine and the law by the creation of national associations and the tightening of requirements for entry into practice. The American Medical Association was founded in 1847, the American Bar Association in 1878. Later on, a bachelor's degree became required for admission to law and medical school.[7] The professionalization of the work that college teachers do is part of this larger context.

Professionalism was born of contradictory impulses. On the one hand, it belongs to the movement toward a democratic society and a free market economy. Professionalism promises to open careers to talent. You can't inherit your occupational status; you have to earn it through some credentialing process in which every entrant is treated equally. Professionalism is also an extension of the division of labor, which is a characteristic of market economies, to the higher-status occupations. Advanced economies generate tasks that call for more

---

[7] This reform was discussed in chapter one.

specific knowledge than one person can possibly acquire, and professionalization is a mechanism for producing the specialized experts who are needed to perform those tasks.

On the other hand, professions are monopolistic: people who don't have the credential can't practice the trade. This monopolistic aspect of professionalization is clearly a reaction against the principles of the free market. Every profession has a side that is turned away from the anarchy of open competition—away from the system that the profession serves and that made professionalization necessary in the first place. Requiring that people earn a credential before they can be allowed to work in one's business is a way of defending oneself and one's fellow practitioners from market forces. In fact, the necessity of avoiding the destabilizing effects of the free market is part of every rationale offered for professionalization in the sociological literature at the turn of the nineteenth century—it is found in Emile Durkheim's *The Social Division of Labor*, in Herbert Croly's *The Promise of American Life*, and in R. H. Tawney's *The Acquisitive Society*.[8] The praise of professionalism was part of a progressive politics in the early years of the twentieth century: Croly was a key figure in progressive circles, a supporter of the trust-buster Theodore Roosevelt and one of the founders of *The New Republic*. All these books argue that the protection that professions afford against market forces is the only way of elevating excellence above profits in a capitalist economy. In

[8] Émile Durkheim, *De la division du travail social* (Paris: F. Alcan, 1893); Herbert Croly, *The Promise of American Life* (New York: Macmillan, 1910); R. H. Tawney, *The Acquisitive Society* (New York: Harcourt, Brace and Howe, 1920). See also Herbert Spencer, *The Principles of Sociology* (New York: Appleton, 1896), Vol. 3, pp. 179–324.

a system that is designed to be driven by efficiency and self-interest, professions set standards for performance that rate quality above dollars. Professionals are people who behave not self-interestedly (as other economic actors theoretically do) but disinterestedly. Doctors sacrifice short-term gains—by, for example, not performing unnecessary operations—in the interests of "good medicine." The reward for their unselfishness is permission to work in a protected market; and since entrance to that market is controlled, professionals usually command superior wages and a high degree of job security. By agreeing to forego the windfalls they could enjoy if they exploited their privileged positions, professionals take their gains over the long term.

Two features of professionalism are supposed to make disinterestedness possible. One is the autonomy of the professional organization. Professions are largely self-regulating: they set the standards for entrance and performance in their specialized areas, and they do so by the light of what is good for the profession rather than what market conditions or external forces, such as legislators or citizens' groups, demand. The American Medical Association exists, among other reasons, to insist that the standard of care not be compromised in response to financial considerations, just as the American Association of University Professors exists to insist that academic freedom not be compromised in response to political considerations. Since professionals are mostly rewarded (or disciplined) according to standards internal to the profession, they have to adhere, most of the time, only to professional standards.

The second feature of professionalism that is supposed to ensure disinterestedness is the very act of specialization itself. Specialization makes work more productive because it narrows the field and therefore allows it to be more deeply and expertly mastered. In Adam Smith's famous example, the worker who pulls the wire in the manufacture of pins pulls it more efficiently for not having spread himself thin by mastering the very different art of affixing the heads.[9] But specialization also performs a profoundly important social function. For the idea behind it is that the knowledge and skills needed for a particular specialized endeavor are transmissible but not transferable. The transmissibility is what makes it possible for the professions to monopolize the production of future professionals. Professions reproduce themselves by passing professional acquirements along from one generation to the next. Professionals are trained by other professionals. People with JDs educate future JDs. The non-transferability of the credential, though, ensures that competence in one profession can never be exercised in another profession. Lawyers cannot treat patients in a hospital and physicians cannot represent clients in a courtroom. People with doctorates in English do not get to decide who deserves a doctorate in sociology. This non-transferability of expertise is the balance wheel of professionalized economies: it prevents excessive claims to authority being made by well-educated people. It provides a check to the elitism inherent in any market-circumventing system. Professionalism is a way of using smart people productively without giving them too much social power.

It is easy to see how the modern academic discipline reproduces all the salient features of the professionalized occupation. It is a self-governing and largely closed community of

---

[9] Adam Smith, *An Inquiry into the Nature and Causes of the Wealth of Nations* (1776), ed. Edwin Cannan (New York: Modern Library, 1937), pp. 3–4.

practitioners who have an almost absolute power to determine the standards for entry, promotion, and dismissal in their fields. The discipline relies on the principle of disinterestedness, according to which the production of new knowledge is regulated by measuring it against existing scholarship through a process of peer review, rather than by the extent to which it meets the needs of interests external to the field. The history department does not ask the mayor or the alumni or the physics department who is qualified to be a history professor. The academic credential is non-transferable (as every PhD looking for work outside the academy quickly learns). And disciplines encourage—in fact, they more or less require—a high degree of specialization. The return to the disciplines for this method of organizing themselves is social authority: the product is guaranteed by the expertise the system is designed to create. Incompetent practitioners are not admitted to practice, and incompetent scholarship is not disseminated.

Since it is the system that ratifies the product—ipso facto, no one outside the community of experts is qualified to rate the value of the work produced within it—the most important function of the system is not the production of knowledge. It is the reproduction of the system. To put it another way, the most important function of the system, both for purposes of its continued survival and for purposes of controlling the market for its products, is the production of the producers. The academic disciplines effectively monopolize (or attempt to monopolize) the production of knowledge in their fields, and they monopolize the production of knowledge producers as well. This is why, for example, you cannot take a course in the law (apart from legal history) outside a law school. In fact, law schools urge applicants to major in areas outside the law. They say that this makes lawyers well rounded, but it also helps to ensure that future lawyers will be trained only by other lawyers. It helps lawyers retain a monopoly on knowledge of the law.

Weirdly, the less social authority a profession enjoys, the more restrictive the barriers to entry and the more rigid the process of producing new producers tend to become. You can become a lawyer in three years, an MD in four years, and an MD-PhD in six years, but the median time to a doctoral degree in the humanities disciplines is nine years.[10]And the more self-limiting the profession, the harder it is to acquire the credential and enter into practice, and the tighter the identification between the individual practitioner and the discipline.

Disciplines are self-regulating in this way for good academic freedom reasons. The system of credentialing and specialization maintains quality and protects people within the field from being interfered with by external forces. The system has enormous benefits, *but only for the professionals*. The weakest professional, because he or she is backed by the collective authority of the group, has an almost unassailable advantage over the strongest non-professional (the so-called independent scholar) operating alone, since the non-professional must build a reputation by his or her own toil, while the professional's credibility is given by the institution. That is one of the reasons that people are willing to pay the enormous price in time and income forgone it takes to get the degree: the credential gives them access to the resources

---

[10] Median total time to degree in the humanities in 2003 was 11.3 years; it was nine years as a registered student. Thomas B. Hoffer and Vincent Welch, Jr., "Time to Degree of U.S. Research Doctorate Recipients," *InfoBrief, Science Resources Statistics* (National Science Foundation, March 2006) pp. 2–3. The significance of the time to degree is discussed later, in chapter four.

of scholarship and to the networks of scholars that circulate their work around the world. The non-academic writer or scholar is largely deprived of those things. This double motive—ensuring quality by restricting access—is reflected in the argument all professions offer as their justification: in order to serve the needs of others properly, professions must be accountable only to themselves.

There is one more stage in the evolution of the modern professional. This is when the institutional piece drops out of the formal picture. Stanley Fish calls this the anti-professionalism that is a requisite part of being an academic professional.[11] Being an academic professional means— often, although by no means always—maintaining a skeptical, sometimes antagonistic relation to the institutional and organizational apparat that credentializes and supports you. It involves internalizing the autonomy that the system makes possible—making the autonomy of the discipline seem your own. The way in which this final bit of transcendence is managed is crucial to understanding the condition of academic professionalism, and hence the condition of disciplinarity, today.

3.

As an illustration of this process, we can use the example of my own discipline, which is English, keeping in mind that although bureaucratically all disciplines are treated alike—

---

[11] Stanley Fish, "Anti-Professionalism," *Doing What Comes Naturally: Change, Rhetoric, and the Practice of Theory in Literary and Legal Studies* (Durham, NC: Duke University Press, 1989), pp. 214–46.

they have parallel requirements for the doctoral degree, for peer review, for tenure, and so on—it is just common sense to acknowledge that some kinds of research fit comfortably within an academic structure and some kinds don't. Academic shorthand for this is a distinction between "soft" disciplines and "hard" disciplines, but the terminology is invidious. Another way of slicing the universe of knowledge production would be to say that some disciplines are interested in the way things are, some are interested in how people behave, and some are interested in what things mean. The first kind of inquiry is basically empirical, the third is basically hermeneutical, and the second usually involves some combination of measurement and interpretation. There are empirical aspects to the business of English departments, but the work is mainly hermeneutical—figuring out what things mean. And the results of this labor are obviously more difficult to assess objectively than the results of a chemistry experiment or an analysis of voting behavior are. Beyond attaining the assent (usually provisional, and understood to be so) of other people who are trying to figure out the same things, there is no watertight verification procedure. So a hermeneutical field of study is likely to show more vividly the consequences of professionalization. It is obliged to undergo more contortions.

In the first years of the modern university, the field of English was dominated by philologists—so much so that for many years at Johns Hopkins, the school that served as the model of a research institution in American higher education (it opened in 1876), English was part of the German department.[12]

---

[12] Historical studies drawn upon in what follows include Graff, *Professing Literature*, esp. pp. 121–61, 183–208; Wallace Douglas, "Accidental Institution:

This way of incorporating literature into the structure of the research university was effective because the disciplines were organized around a scientistic conception of scholarship, and philology—the study of language—could clearly lay claim to being scientific. Eventually, philology was superseded by literary history as the dominant scholarly appraisal, but there was still no problem. Literary history, too, could lay the same claim to a scientific, or sciencelike, status. The problem arose when English professors proposed to produce literary criticism.

From a purely intellectual point of view, the obstacles to including literary criticism among the professional activities of English professors are slightly absurd. Literary criticism would seem a natural part of the job description. But there were obstacles, and they were thrown up not by problems most people would otherwise have had with the practice of criticism, but by the design of the institution. In order for literary criticism to be recognized as a valid professional pursuit—that is, an activity amenable to the process of self-regulation that governs the production of academic knowledge—several points needed to be established. The first was that literature is indeed an object that can be isolated for academic inquiry. This meant demonstrating that literature is a field whose study requires a transmissible but untranslatable body of knowledge and skills; that literary criticism, or a

On the Origin of Modern Language Study," in Gerald Graff and Reginald Gibbons, eds., *Criticism in the University* (Evanston, IL: Northwestern University Press, 1985), pp. 35–61; and Wallace Martin, "Criticism and the Academy," in A. Walton Litz, Louis Menand, and Lawrence Rainey, eds., *The Cambridge History of Literary Criticism.* Vol. 7: *Modernism and the New Criticism* (Cambridge: Cambridge University Press, 2000), pp. 269–321. See also Jonathan Culler, "Literary Criticism and the American University," *Framing the Sign: Criticism and Its Institutions* (Oxford: Basil Blackwell, 1988), pp. 3–40.

particular form of literary criticism, constitutes such a body of knowledge and skills; and that proto-specialists in literary studies can be vetted and credentialed by standard academic methods—that is, by the writing of an original contribution to knowledge (a dissertation), by the submission of scholarship to peer-reviewed journals and presses, by tenure review, and all the other machinery of the academic profession.

To the extent that literary criticism is thought of as the possibly idiosyncratic interpretation and appreciation of works of literature and the drawing of moral and other non-aesthetic conclusions from those activities, the university literature department is not especially well suited to the business of producing either interesting literary criticism or interesting literary critics. But to the degree that literary criticism is thought of as a discovery about the nature of literature or of literary language by the application of philosophically grounded methods of inquiry, then the modern academy becomes a relatively congenial place in which to practice criticism. The challenge as it presented itself to literary critics in the first half of the twentieth century is summed up by the literary historian Wallace Martin: "So long as they doggedly insisted on the importance of values and taste, in opposition to the positivistic conception of knowledge defended by the scholars, critics had little to contribute to the institutionalized study of literature. What they opposed, ultimately, was not simply the scholars, but the conception of knowledge on which the modern university is based. In their turn toward principles and theory, they found a means of legitimating criticism as a form of knowledge."[13] This task of professional-

---

[13] Martin, "Criticism and the Academy," p. 273.

izing literary criticism took a long time to perform. The word "criticism" was not added to the Modern Language Association's constitution, which enumerates the objectives of professional literature and language studies, until 1951.[14] A transformation on this scale is a function of many factors operating together, from changes in student demographics to changes in funding. But to pick one prominent intellectual contribution to, or reflection of, the change, we can compare the English scholar George Saintsbury's three-volume *History of Criticism and Literary Taste in Europe*, published from 1900 to 1904, with two great scholarly testaments of the academic New Criticism, René Wellek's multivolume *History of Modern Criticism: 1750–1950*, which began appearing in 1955, and Cleanth Brooks and William K. Wimsatt's not-so-short *Short History of Literary Criticism*, which was published in 1957. (Wellek, Brooks, and Wimsatt were all professors at Yale.) In 1904, Saintsbury, who was a professor of rhetoric at the University of Edinburgh, noted that friends had questioned the point of writing a book called *A History of Criticism and Literary Taste* by asking him whether literature really was something one could talk about as a thing in itself. Saintsbury said that he could only answer those friends by asserting his faith that literature is in fact such a thing, and that there was a history of people doing it.[15]

For the New Critics, who constituted the first generation of literary critics in American English departments, an assertion of faith was not sufficient. Wellek took the trouble in the

[14] Graff, *Professing Literature*, p. 283n.

[15] George Saintsbury, *A History of Criticism and Literary Taste in Europe, from the Earliest Texts to the Present Day* (Edinburgh: Blackwood, 1900–04), Vol. 3, p. vi.

preface to the first volume of his *History of Modern Criticism* to complain that although Saintsbury's history is "admirable in its sweep and still readable because of the liveliness of the author's exposition and style . . . [it] seems to me seriously vitiated by its professed lack of interest in questions of theory and aesthetics." It was Wellek's belief that, as he put it, "the history of criticism is a topic which has its own inherent interest, *even without relation to the history of the practice of writing*,"[16] and it was the purpose of his history to furnish the proof.

Brooks and Wimsatt went further in the *Short History*. What the history of criticism proves, they argued, is not just that literary criticism is a discipline, but that literature itself is a distinctive object of study—that literature is something that can be talked about "as literature," and not as a branch of moral philosophy or social history or the history of ideas. We write, they explain, in the belief that there is "continuity and intelligibility in the history of literary argument. . . . Literary problems occur not just because history produces them, but because literature is a thing of such and such a sort, showing such and such a relation to the history of human experience." What the study of literary criticism opens up, they claim, is "not so many diverse views into multiplicity and chaos but so many complementary insights into the one deeply rooted and perennial human truth which is the poetic principle."[17] This argument—that there is such a thing as specifically lit-

---

[16] René Wellek, *A History of Modern Criticism: 1750–1950* (New Haven: Yale University Press, 1955–66), Vol. 1, pp. vi, 7 (my emphasis).

[17] William K. Wimsatt and Cleanth Brooks, *Literary Criticism: A Short History* (Chicago: University of Chicago Press, 1957), Vol. 1, pp. vii, ix–x.

erary language, and that literary criticism provides an analytical toolbox for examining it—was the basis for the New
Criticism's claim to a place in the structure of the research
university. It justifies the emphasis on the formal properties
of literary texts and the concentration on "close reading" that
characterize New Critical scholarship and pedagogy—an
emphasis that is reiterated right up through the time of the
Yale school of criticism, in the 1970s.[18]

The story of the way literary criticism adjusted to the
requirements of disciplinarity is interesting in the context of
professionalization because of its use of a figure who played
a central role in the process, even though he was not an academic and had little use for academic criticism. This was T. S.
Eliot.[19] Eliot was a hero to the New Critics when they were
young, because of his poetry, his conservative social thought,
and his literary criticism—but also because of his example.
He had gone to England to write his dissertation (he was a
doctoral student in philosophy at Harvard) in 1914, when he

[18] Commonly identified with J. Hillis Miller, Geoffrey Hartman, Paul de Man,
and Harold Bloom, all professors at Yale. Together with Jacques Derrida, who
began teaching regularly at Yale in 1975, they published *Deconstruction and
Criticism* (New York: Continuum, 1979), which gave the world the notion
(slightly mistaken, since Bloom was never a deconstructionist) of a "school."
See Jonathan Arac, Wlad Godzich, and Wallace Martin, eds., *The Yale Critics:
Deconstruction in America* (Minneapolis: University of Minnesota Press, 1983).
Yale was also a bastion of the New Criticism in the fifties. There is a very good
account of the New Critics in Grant Webster, *The Republic of Letters: A History
of Postwar American Literary Opinion* (Baltimore: Johns Hopkins University
Press, 1979), pp. 63–206. On the non-literary aspects of the New Criticism,
see Mark Jancovich, *The Cultural Politics of the New Criticism* (New York: Cambridge University Press, 1993).

[19] I discuss Eliot's relation to academic English studies in "T. S. Eliot and
Modernity," *New England Quarterly*, 69 (1996): 554–79.

was twenty-six and knew almost no one there. Eight years later, he was famous as the author of two of the most spectacular books in twentieth-century poetry, *Prufrock and Other Observations* (1917) and *The Waste Land* (1922), and the editor of his own quarterly journal, *The Criterion*. He had also published one of the seminal collections of critical essays in English studies, *The Sacred Wood* (1920). All of Eliot's criticism, and particularly its tone and special vocabulary, is important to the story; but his most widely cited and reprinted essay, "Tradition and the Individual Talent" (1919), is a powerful statement of the basis for criticism as an autonomous discipline.[20] The question that essay essentially asks is: What does the poet need to know? And the answer it gives is: Poetry. The corollary to this is that the best way to understand poems is by their relation to other poems. This is a premise without which the enterprise of academic literary criticism would be unable to function.

Eliot's prescription is a formalism, and so is academic disciplinarity. That is, it isolates one aspect of experience and makes that aspect the basis for an autonomous field of inquiry that can be legitimately pursued without special knowledge of any other field of inquiry. English professors need not be historians, sociologists, psychologists, or philosophers to be regarded as full-fledged contributing professionals. They need no training or credentials in those fields (and, usually, they have none). They can be historians, critics, and theorists of literature knowing, in their professional capacity, only literature.

[20] T. S. Eliot, "Tradition and the Individual Talent," *The Sacred Wood* (London: Methuen, 1920), pp. 47–59.

This stage, in which a new practice is incorporated into the academic institution by providing a theoretical justification for its autonomy, is followed by a final move, which is the erasure of the historical boundary between the professional era (the era of the research university) and the pre-professional era—in the case of literary criticism, the era of the amateur, the man of letters. In the history of English studies, Eliot was the key figure. He was a critic who was never associated with an academic institution, but who produced a criticism whose vocabulary and criteria for judgment were scientistic-sounding, and which could be appropriated by academics without betraying their personal or political interests or ad hoc motivations (which Eliot himself certainly had plenty of: he was trying, in his critical essays, to promote his own poetry). Between the non-academic literary universe of Keats, Arnold, and Wilde and the academic literary universe of the Yale English department, Eliot was the link. Thus Wellek's *History of Modern Criticism* begins with Immanuel Kant and ends, many volumes later, with Wellek's Yale colleague, William Wimsatt. And thus Harvard professor Walter Jackson Bate's widely used anthology of literary criticism begins with Plato and ends with *his* colleague, Douglas Bush, as though there were no meaningful situational distinction between the two figures.[21] The anthology, in fact, is the principal instrument by which this elision between the pre- and post-professional eras is performed. So that we get, for example, an anthology of political philosophy that includes Jean-Jacques Rousseau and the Harvard philosopher John Rawls, or an anthology

[21] Walter Jackson Bate, *Criticism: The Major Texts* (New York: Harcourt, Brace, 1952).

of art criticism that includes Charles Baudelaire and the art history professor Rosalind Krauss.

This final step is necessary because the professional organizations and institutions and associations that emerged to control and protect the production of knowledge producers become too visible. They make too easy a target, and the individual practitioner who borrows their credibility also takes on the problem of how to distance herself from those "official" positions she finds inconvenient or unacceptable—but without losing their authority. In a profession in which freedom of thought is both a matter of intense piety and an institutional mechanism for maintaining professional autonomy, the ability to identify with something beyond official organizations and institutions and even disciplines is a pressing one. Academics don't want to appear to be conformists: their success depends on it.

The consummation of the professional project therefore occurs not when the professional association has achieved independence from outside control, but when the association is no longer perceived as the true source of the professional's authority. Though we expect the lawyer to have been certified by all the appropriate institutions, his social status derives from the sense of his belonging not to the Bar Association (regarded as a trivial job requirement, particularly by those who already belong) but to the ancient profession of the law. Professions create traditions that exceed their own histories. They do this, again, by isolating a feature of the practice (it can be more than one feature, of course) that requires special attention—in the case of English studies, for example, understanding literary language; in the case of the law, thinking like a lawyer—and they make attention to this feature the chief criterion for determining whether the practice is done properly or not. The profession then forms a canon based on this construction. And by this means, the profession achieves the appearance of tradition and continuity in a social and economic formation—ours— that is characterized principally by change.

4.

After the 1960s, something happened to many of the academic disciplines: a relatively boundary-respecting conception of scholarly inquiry gave way to a relatively boundary-suspicious conception. This coincided, unsurprisingly, with a loss of respect for professional authority in society as a whole. The historian Thomas Haskell has noted that he could find almost nothing negative written about professionalism in the social science literature before 1939; the sociologist Eliot Freidson says that there is almost nothing positive after 1960.[22] The public began to distrust experts and professionals—or, at least, professionalism. Of course, there has been a large increase in the number of professional degrees awarded since 1960 (one consequence of the growth in the higher education system), but the professionalization of everyone and everything is perfectly consistent with the demise of professional authority.

In some fields, the paradigms got broken and were not ever really repaired. English or anthropology is today the study of

---

[22] Thomas Haskell, "Professionalism *versus* Capitalism: R. H. Tawney, Émile Durkheim, and C. S. Peirce on the Disinterestedness of Professional Communities," and Eliot Freidson, "Are Professions Necessary?," in Haskell, ed., *The Authority of Experts: Studies in History and Theory* (Bloomington: Indiana University Press, 1984), pp. 182, 4–5. See also Walter Metzger, "A Spectre Is Haunting American Scholars: The Spectre of 'Professionism,'" *Educational Researcher*, vol. 16, no. 6 (1987): 10–19.

what, exactly? If, fifty years ago, you asked a dozen anthropology professors what anthropology's program of inquiry was—what anthropology professors did that distinguished them from history professors, sociology professors, economics professors, and psychology professors—you might have gotten different and even contradictory answers. But by and large the professors would have had little trouble filling in the blank in the sentence, Anthropology is ____. If they did have trouble, they would not have boasted about it. Today, you would be likely to get two types of answer. One answer is: Anthropology is the study of its own assumptions. The other answer is: Anthropology is whatever people in anthropology departments do. Not every discipline thinks of itself like this, but that is another result of skepticism toward disciplinarity: it is spread unevenly across academic departments. This heightens the worry that professors in different fields are no longer talking with one another, and thus raises the stakes for interdisciplinarity. Part of the promise of interdisciplinarity is that it will smooth out the differences between the empirical and the hermeneutic, the hard and the soft, disciplines. "If we could just get them in the same room together . . ."

Anti-disciplinarity—the position that since disciplines exclude certain approaches and subject matters, scholars need to work in opposition to them—is an unsustainable paradigm. It begins as a backlash, but as soon as it generates productive work, it can readily be folded into the home discipline by the standard academic practice of adding on. And, in any event, the disciplines still control the production and placement of new professors, and the advent in some fields of a kind of post-disciplinarity does not necessarily mean that departments are obsolete. They still possess the credentialing power and the hiring power, and even if they are losing intellectual respect, it is not at all clear that it is in the interests of the faculty to have them wither away. For one of the functions they perform is the preservation of academic freedom. The discipline acts as the community that judges its members' work by community standards. When professors can be hired on an ad hoc basis by administrators, or when they are not professionally situated within a department, they can lose some of this protection. Their status becomes a function of lines in a budget. Administrators (at least in theory) would love to melt down the disciplines, since that would allow universities to deploy faculty more efficiently. Why support medievalists in the history department, the English department, the French and German departments, and the art history department, none of them probably attracting huge enrollments, when you can hire one supermedievalist and install her in a Medieval Studies program, whose survival can be made to depend in part on its ability to attract outside funding?

Which brings us back to interdisciplinarity. Interdisciplinarity is not something different from disciplinarity. It is the ratification of the logic of disciplinarity. In practice, it actually tends to rigidify disciplinary paradigms. A typical interdisciplinary situation might bring together, in a classroom, a literature professor and an anthropologist. The role of the literature professor is to perform qua literature professor, bringing to bear the specialized methods and knowledge of literary study to the subject at hand; the role of the anthropologist is to do the same with the methods of anthropological inquiry. This methodological contrast is regarded as, in fact, the intellectual and pedagogical takeaway of the collaboration. What happens is the phenomenon of borrowed authority: the literature professor can incorporate into his work the insights of the anthropologist, in the form of "As anthropology has shown us," ignoring the probability that the particular insight being recognized is highly contested within the anthropologist's own discipline.

Because professors are trained to respect the autonomy and expertise of other disciplines, they are rarely in a position to evaluate one another's claims. So there is nothing transgressive about interdisciplinarity on this description. There is nothing even new about it. Disciplinarity has not only been ratified; it has been fetishized. The disciplines are treated as the sum of all possible perspectives. One of the benefits that is hoped for from interdisciplinarity, especially in the classroom, is that differing perspectives will provide mutual critiques—that putting an economist in the same classroom as a psychologist and an art historian will give students a sense of the limits of each academic enterprise. This seems a little wishful, as though the process can be automatically self-correcting. Critique is the beginning of correction, it's true, but the aim of knowledge is not only to recognize limitations. The aim is also to transcend them.

In the humanities, where talk of interdisciplinarity is most common, these practices tend to reinforce the Balkanized structure of knowledge production that universities inherited from the nineteenth century. This is the structure that divides literature by nationality and the arts by medium. It is a retrograde way to teach the humanities, but it is hard to see how interdisciplinarity per se can do more than mildly ameliorate it. Professors are still trained in one national literature or artistic medium or another. In an interdisciplinary encounter, they just shout at each other from the mountaintops of their own disciplines. For, as we have already seen, the key to professional transformation is not at the level of knowledge production. It is at the level of professional reproduction. Until professors are produced in a different way, the structure of academic knowledge production and dissemination is unlikely to change significantly.

5.

The professionalization of higher education was a perfectly reasonable development. It was consistent with the transformation of higher-status occupations generally after 1870, and it served many interests well. Among other things, it made research the main mission of higher education, a change reflected in the statistic that between 1920 and 1950, undergraduate enrollment increased by a factor of ten, but graduate enrollment increased by a factor of fifty.[23] What is significant about the post-1960s backlash against professionalism and disciplinarity is that it was not accompanied by a loosening of the requirements for admission to and promotion within the academic profession. On the contrary: the road to a professorship is much steeper than it was fifty years ago. Even as late as 1969, a third of American professors did not have PhDs.[24] Today, the PhD is a virtually universal prerequisite for professorial appointment. And the discourse of the pro-

---

[23] Peter M. Blau, *The Organization of Academic Work* (New York: Wiley, 1973), p. 5.

[24] Ibid., p. 27. Figures cited by David Damrosch. For speculation on some of the consequences, see Damrosch, *We Scholars: Changing the Culture of the University* (Cambridge, MA: Harvard University Press, 1995), esp. pp. 24–47.

fessoriate has become national and disciplinary, not local and institutional—another characteristic of professionalization. In 1989, 40 percent of professors reported that they felt loyalty to their institution; 70 percent said that they felt loyalty to their discipline.[25] We can assume that this sense of identity is a function of another statistic: in 1969, 21 percent of professors agreed with the statement that it would be difficult to get tenure in their departments without publications; in 1989, 42 percent of professors agreed with that statement.[26] One of the reasons it is difficult to establish interdisciplinarity locally is that there is little interdisciplinarity nationally, and professors regard institutional initiatives as provisional and as unrelated to career advancement, which comes from recognition at the national level.

So, what is the fascination with interdisciplinarity all about? The art critic Harold Rosenberg once published a book called *The Anxious Object*.[27] The title was a reference to the art of the sixties—Pop Art, Minimalism, and Conceptual Art. Rosenberg thought that those art objects were anxious because they were uncertain of their own identity. They kept asking themselves questions like, Am I a work of art, or just a wall of Polaroids? Am I a sculpture, or just a pile of bricks? More existentially: Am I an autotelic aesthetic artifact, or just a commercial good?

---

[25] Ernest Boyer, *Scholarship Reconsidered: Priorities of the Professoriate* (San Francisco: Carnegie Foundation for the Advancement of Teaching, 1990), p. 56.

[26] Ibid., p. 12.

[27] Harold Rosenberg, *The Anxious Object: Art Today and Its Audience* (New York: Horizon, 1964), esp. pp. 13–20.

What causes anxiety to break out in a work of art? Self-consciousness. Maybe, in the case of the academic subject, self-consciousness about disciplinarity and about the status of the professor—the condition whose genealogy I have been sketching in this chapter—is a source of anxiety. That status just seems to keep reproducing itself; there is no way out of the institutional process. And this leads the academic to ask questions like, Am I an individual disinterested inquirer, or a cog in a knowledge machine? And, Am I questioning the status quo, or am I reproducing it? More existentially, Is my relation to the living culture that of a creator or that of a packager? The only way to get past the anxiety these questions cause is to get past the questions—to see that they are bad questions because they require people to choose between identities that cannot be separated. A work of art is *both* an aesthetic object and a commercial good. That is not a contradiction unless you have been socialized to believe that it must be.

Academics have been trained to believe that there must be a contradiction between being a scholar or an intellectual and being part of a system of socialization. They are conditioned to think that their workplace does not operate like a market, even as they compete with one another for status and advantage. Most of all, they are ambivalent about the status they have worked so hard to achieve. Interdisciplinary anxiety is a displaced anxiety about the position of privilege that academic professionalism confers on its initiates *and* about the peculiar position of social disempowerment created by the barrier between academic workers and the larger culture. It is an anxiety about the formalism and methodological fetishism of the disciplines *and* about the danger of sliding into an aimless subjectivism or eclecticism. It is an anxiety about the institutional co-optation of innovation *and* about institutional indifference or hostility to the new. Professors have become skeptical of the rhetoric of disinterestedness, but they are also contemptuous of claims of advocacy.[28]

Existentially (and here I am speaking very subjectively, but anxiety is subjective, *fear* is objective), I think that anxiety about interdisciplinarity is an expression of frustration. Academics of my generation grew up in a period—the sixties and seventies—when the world of art and ideas was undergoing changes that seemed to be coming from way outside the box of received ideas and methods. I think that many of us hoped to instantiate something like that ad hoc, performative mode of pedagogy and inquiry within the university, to strike out in new directions, to break down the walls a little. We believed that we could shake off the effects of our academic socialization, in part by theorizing about them. The theorizing was successful (I just rehearsed some of it here), but the shaking off did not happen quite as we had dreamed it might. Of course, professors in my generation are now relatively secure in our domains. But is it possible that we envy a little those contributors to the culture who have to do battle with the forces of the market and with heteronomy—with the reality checks of life outside the university? I think we might be. I think we want to contribute to the culture and the society that is being created and lived all around us, and we are a little sick of the institutional armature we once may have desired to secure us.

Mainly, we want to feel we are in a real fight, a fight not

---

[28] See the essays in Patricia Meyer Spacks, ed., *Advocacy in the Classroom: Problems and Possibilities* (New York: St. Martin's Press, 1996).

with each other and our schools, which is the fight that outsiders seem to be encouraging us to have, but with the forces that make and remake the world most human beings live in. We want to bring the dissonance and the struggles of competing interests, the risks of innovation and experimentation, into our box, and we are scandalized that the box refuses to accommodate them. It's true that the box was designed with an entirely different intellectual game in mind. It was designed to protect professors and their valuable socializing function from the beasts of political and commercial interests. But those beasts are out there. They are what make the fight real. Maybe not all of the problem is with the box. "You tell me it's the institution," the song says. The institution is not inherently a friend to innovation and transgression and creativity. But it is not inherently an enemy, either. Interdisciplinarity is an administrative name for an anxiety and a hope that are personal.

4

Why Do Professors
All Think Alike?

1.

THE POLITICS of professors has been an issue in higher education since the end of the nineteenth century. And why shouldn't it be? Professors enjoy social authority, they virtually monopolize the business of knowledge production in many areas, and they have intimate and largely unsupervised access to developing minds. Their political views are important. At the same time, it is a custom in the modern university to segregate those views from the professional identities of professors—that is, to treat views extraneous to the subject matter of teaching and scholarship as somehow "out of bounds" to the evaluation of job performance. We don't approve when the chemistry professor gives anti-war speeches (or pro-war speeches, for that matter) in chemistry class, and we may intervene, because we feel that the professor has impermissibly mixed her politics and her job. But we choose to not make it a problem when she gives such speeches out in the quad or on the street.

Professors have the protection of this firewall as part of a deal more or less tacitly worked out at the time of the establishment of the American Association of University

Professors in 1915.[1] The AAUP was founded to articulate and defend the principle of academic freedom in the wake of several notorious cases in which professors were fired for expressing political views that trustees or administrators considered obnoxious. The principle of academic freedom was designed to allow professors to pursue inquiry wherever it leads, without fear of damaging their careers if they reach results other people find offensive. It is, in effect, a pact with the rest of society: the results of academic inquiry will be worthwhile if professors are held immune from sanctions for the political implications of their work and for their personal political views. But another reason for the principle of academic freedom is that it helped to define academic inquiry as, by its nature, a value-neutral enterprise. Protecting professors' political and religious views was a way underscoring their irrelevance to research and teaching. The modern university was about knowledge, not ideology. It was about facts, not values. It should have been obvious that patrolling this distinction was going to be a never-ending task.

It did not seem so at first, at least to John Dewey, the Columbia philosopher who (with Arthur Lovejoy) was the founder of the AAUP and who became its first president. When he took office, Dewey said that he imagined that within a few years, cases involving violations of professors' academic freedom would be rare—a comment that gives an idea of the irenic nature of Dewey's mind. Characteristically, he was too optimistic, and by the end of the year, he had

---

[1] The classic history is Richard Hofstadter and Walter P. Metzger, *The Development of Academic Freedom in the United States* (New York: Columbia University Press, 1955).

to admit that he had been mistaken.[2] Professors' politics are usually a low-level issue in higher education. They become a high-level, and sometimes inflammatory, issue during times of public anxiety: during turn-of-the-century debates over immigration, for example, or when the United States entered the First World War. The politics of professors was an issue during the McCarthy period in the early Cold War, and at the time of the protests against the war in Vietnam. They became an issue in the so-called culture wars in the late 1980s, and again after the attacks of September 11, 2001.

Almost all professors subscribe to the principle of academic freedom under a fairly non-restrictive interpretation, and they are right to do so. Faculty members are by nature contentious and inefficient self-governors, but faculties must govern themselves. Simply as a practical matter, experience shows that you cannot dictate to tenured professors, or put their feet to the fire of public opinion, with much hope of success. Administrators come and go, but tenure is forever. But the importance of the principle goes beyond that. Academic freedom is not just a nice job perk. It is the philosophical key to the whole enterprise of higher education.[3] It informs more than the odd case of the professor who writes articles that can be read as promoting man-boy love or as condoning ter-

---

[2] John Dewey, "Introductory Address to the American Association of University Professors," January 1, 1915, and "Annual Address of the President to the American Association of University Professors," December 15, 1915, both in *The Middle Works, 1899–1924*, ed. Jo Ann Boydston (Carbondale, IL: Southern Illinois University Press, 1976–83), Vol. 8, pp. 98–108.

[3] I discuss the role of the principle of academic freedom in "The Limits of Academic Freedom," in Louis Menand, ed., *The Future of Academic Freedom* (Chicago: University of Chicago Press, 1996), pp. 3–20.

rorism.[4] It includes practices and customs such as the inability of the football coach to influence the quarterback's grade in math class. It gives academics a (circumscribed) zone of autonomy in which to work.

The claim by conservatives that the academy is under the control of a left-wing professoriate is an old one, and studies since the fifties have tended to confirm the general suspicion that professors, as a group, are more liberal than the general public. In 1952, for example, social science professors voted for Adlai Stevenson over Dwight Eisenhower in the presidential election by a margin of 58 percent to 30 percent, even though Eisenhower (who, when he ran for office, was the president of Columbia University) won the election by almost 11 percentage points.[5] Stevenson was not exactly Ho Chi Minh, though. He was, by the standards of only a decade later, quite conservative on issues like race relations and women's rights. It was after the campus protests of the sixties—over free speech, civil rights, the draft, and the war in Vietnam—that the notion of the professoriate as a group of tenured radicals became dominant in the discourse of the culture wars.[6] That charge was revived after September 11 by critics outside the academy, such as David Horowitz (who was

---

[4] These are references to actual cases, at the University of Missouri–Kansas City, involving Harris Mirkin, in 2002, and at the University of Colorado at Boulder, involving Ward Churchill, in 2005.

[5] Paul F. Lazersfeld and Wagner Thielens, Jr., *The Academic Mind: Social Scientists in a Time of Crisis* (Glencoe, IL: The Free Press, 1958), p. 14.

[6] Roger Kimball, *Tenured Radicals: How Politics Has Corrupted Our Higher Education* (New York: Harper & Row, 1990). A similar, bestselling account from the same period is Dinesh D'Souza, *Illiberal Education: The Politics of Race and Sex on Campus* (New York: The Free Press, 1991).

once an untenured radical himself, but by 2001 had become an activist against academic leftism),[7] and there have been a few surveys—from a social scientific point of view rather sketchy ones—done to support it.[8]

In 2007, two sociologists working at Harvard and George Mason, Neil Gross and Solon Simmons, conducted a national survey of the political views of the professoriate that observed all the protocols of scientific research and that has a good claim to being an accurate statistical picture of the views of the 630,000 full-time professors, at every level of institution, from research universities to community colleges, in the United States at the time.[9] (Gross and Simmons did not include part-time faculty in their survey, although they note

[7] David Horowitz and Eli Lehrer, "Political Bias in the Administrations and Faculties of 32 Elite Colleges and Universities" (San Francisco: Center for the Study of Popular Culture, 2002). Horowitz sponsors a related Web site, www.studentsforacademicfreedom.org.

[8] Daniel Klein and Andrew Western, "Voter Registration of Berkeley and Stanford Faculty," *Academic Questions*, 18 (2004–05): 53–65; Klein and Charlotta Stern, "Political Diversity in Six Disciplines," *Academic Questions*, 18 (2004–05): 40–52; Stanley Rothman, S. Robert Lichter, and Neil Nevitte, "Politics and Professional Advancement Among College Faculty," *The Forum*, vol. 3, no. 1 (2005), article 2; Gary A. Tobin and Aryeh K. Weinberg, "A Profile of American College Faculty: Political Beliefs and Behavior" (San Francisco: Institute for Jewish and Community Research, 2006); and John F. Zipp and Rudy Fenwick, "Is the Academy a Liberal Hegemony? The Political Orientations and Educational Values of Professors," *Public Opinion Quarterly*, 70 (2006): 304–26. The methodologies of these surveys are critiqued in Gross and Simmons, cited in note 9 below.

[9] Neil Gross and Solon Simmons, "The Social and Political Views of American Professors" (2007), working paper, at http://www.wjh.harvard.edu/~ngross/lounsbery_9-25.pdf. The survey was supported by a grant from the Richard Lounsbery Foundation and was the subject of a conference, "The Politics of the Professors," at Harvard University in 2007. I was a principal investigator on the grant and involved in the construction of the questionnaire; I was not

that about 47 percent of college instruction in the United States is done by part-timers. Assessing the views of part-time faculty presents methodological challenges, but of course those views are relevant to an understanding of politics in academic life.) The results of the survey are quite stunning.

2.

Gross and Simmons argue that the significant finding in their survey is that professors are not as radical as some critics have charged: 9.4 percent of American professors identify themselves as "extremely liberal" (only 3 percent of professors say they are Marxists) and 13.5 percent of faculty describe themselves as "liberal activists." These self-reports are meaningful because professors demonstrate a much greater degree of ideological constraint in their views than most people do. That is, if professors say that they are liberals, their views on specific issues will be coherently and consistently liberal views.[10] In the general population, most people do not know what it means to identify themselves as liberals or conservatives. People will report themselves to be liberals in an opinion poll and then answer specific questions with views normally thought of as conservative. People also give inconsistent answers to the same questions over time. This is because most people are not ideologues—they don't

---

involved in the administration of the survey or the analysis of the results. The data I draw on are from the working paper and are still subject to review.

[10] Gross and Simmons used a number of measures to confirm the self-reporting: for example, they correlated answers to survey questions about political persuasion and political party with views on specific issues, such as the war in Iraq, abortion, homosexual relations, and so on.

have coherent political belief systems—and their views on the issues do not hang together. Their reporting is not terribly accurate.[11] But academics do tend to be ideologues, in this social science sense, so if less than 10 percent of them identify themselves as "extremely liberal," that is a relatively reliable finding. If more than 90 percent of full-time faculty are not "extremely liberal," then academia is not dominated by people with radical political views.

Gross and Simmons also found that, contrary to some assumptions, the more elite the institution, the less likely the professors there are to be left-wing. Professors at liberal arts colleges are much more to the left than professors at PhD-granting institutions. This is interesting, since the education and socialization of professors at liberal arts colleges and professors at research universities is usually identical: they are trained in the same graduate programs and are hired from the same pool. It suggests some institutional treatment effects in a realm where most of the results suggest selection effects (as we will discuss later). Gross and Simmons found that younger professors today tend to be more moderate in their political views than older professors, supporting the theory that the generation that entered the professoriate in the sixties was a spike on the chart ideologically. They also found, however, that younger professors are more liberal in their social views. But the most important finding of the survey, they say, is that a large plurality of professors holds a center-left politics. Most professors are

[11] The classic study, whose results have been much confirmed, is Philip Converse, "The Nature of Belief Systems in Mass Publics," in David Apter, ed., *Ideology and Discontent* (Glencoe, IL: The Free Press, 1964), pp. 206–61.

not Ralph Naderites or socialists; they are mainstream liberal Democrats—at the time of the survey, John Kerry supporters.

What is striking about these results is not the finding that professors tend to be mainstream liberals. It is the finding that they are so *overwhelmingly* mainstream liberals. These are the data:

Political Orientation	Percentage
Extremely liberal	9.4
Liberal	34.7
Slightly liberal	18.1
Middle-of-the-road	18.0
Slightly conservative	10.5
Conservative	8.0
Very conservative	1.2[12]

This means that 62.2 percent of the professoriate is some kind of liberal; only 19.7 percent is some kind of conservative. Collapsing this to a three-point scale—merging the slightly liberal and the slightly conservative with the middle-of-the-roads—we get: 44.1 percent of professors are liberal and 9.2 percent are conservative. By contrast, in the public opinion poll closest to the time of the survey, the American public as a whole reported itself to be 23.3 percent liberal and 31.9 percent conservative.[13]

[12] These and subsequent data are from Gross and Simmons's working paper. When the numbers do not add up to 100, it is due to rounding.

[13] Data from 2004. Liberal-Conservative self-identification 1972–2004, *ANES Guide to Public Opinion and Electoral Behavior*, at http://www.electionstudies .org/nesguide/toptable/tab3_1.htm.

There are differences in the distribution of political views as one moves up and down the higher education hierarchy, but the distribution is surprisingly consistent across the liberal arts divisions. (Gross and Simmons did not include professors at professional schools in their study.)

Field	Liberal (%)	Moderate (%)	Conservative (%)
Natural sciences	45.2	47.0	7.8
Social sciences	58.2	36.9	4.9
Humanities	52.5	44.3	3.6

Outside the liberal arts fields—in health, business, and computer science and engineering—liberals and conservatives are about equally distributed, with more professors identifying themselves as moderates than as either liberal or conservative. Overall, professors skew Democratic: 51 percent call themselves Democrats and 35.3 percent say they are independents, with most of these leaning Democratic. Only 13.7 percent of professors identify themselves as Republicans. In the public at large, in 2006, 34.3 percent of the population identified themselves as Democrats and 30.4 percent as Republicans.[14] In the 2004 presidential election, George Bush won 50.7 percent of the vote and John Kerry won 48.2 percent; 77.6 percent of professors voted for Kerry, 20.4 percent for Bush.

These statistics reflect the views of large samples of the professoriate—all natural scientists at every type of institution, for example. When you begin to crunch the data more finely, you find more extreme skewing: 51 percent of English profes-

[14] Gallup poll cited in Gross and Simmons.

sors are Democrats, for example, and 2 percent are Republicans. In history departments, 3.8 percent of professors are Republicans; 79.2 percent are Democrats. Only 5.5 percent of sociologists and 6.3 percent of political scientists are Republicans. At elite institutions, only 9.5 percent of professors in all fields are Republicans; over 60 percent are Democrats. The statistical breakdown of faculty voting patterns in the 2004 presidential election is fairly striking. At elite colleges and universities, 95 percent of social science professors voted for Kerry; the rest voted for third-party candidates. Zero percent (statistically) voted for Bush. More than 95 percent of humanities professors at elite institutions voted for Kerry, 0 percent for Bush.

There are a number of explanations for why academics are significantly more liberal than the rest of the population. There is a high correlation between education and liberal social and political views, for one thing. For another, professors are trained to question the status quo, so they are less likely to be conservative to the extent that conservatism means resistance to change. (Of course, for this explanation to be consistent, one would expect that in an environment in which liberalism *is* the status quo, many professors might choose not to identify themselves as liberals. This does not seem to be the case.) There may be fewer institutional havens for left-wing intellectuals than there are for right-wing intellectuals, so liberals tend to congregate in universities, conservatives elsewhere—in foundations or, during the years of the Bush administration, in Washington.

It also may be the case that people with conservative views generally find work in the for-profit sector more congenial than people with liberal views do. A recent survey done by two political scientists suggests that young people with conservative views are more likely to seek careers outside academia because they value making money and/or having a family more highly than liberal young people do.[15] And there are possible demographic explanations: as Gross and Simmons point out, younger cohorts in the professoriate are significantly more moderate politically than the baby boom cohort. So the left-wing skewing may continue to moderate as baby boomers move out of the system. What this means, though, is that the professoriate will become even *less* ideologically diverse than it is today, since there will be shrinkage on the far left of the political spectrum. The radicals will die or retire and opinion will regress toward the mean—which is to say, the ideology of the center-liberal Democrat.

Possibly more pressing is the question whether holding liberal views has become a tacit requirement for entry and promotion in the academic profession. This issue has a number of aspects. One has to do with the way in which class cuts across the distribution of political and social views among the professoriate. Gross and Simmons note that "preliminary regression analysis suggests that it is the lower average levels of educational attainment and lower social class origins of conservative and Republican academics that may do the most to account for their underrepresentation in elite research institutions." In other words, a conservative who goes into academic life is likely to start lower down in the educational hierarchy than a liberal, and may therefore have a harder time

---

[15] See Robin Wilson, "Conservatives Just Aren't into Academe, Study Finds," *Chronicle of Higher Education*, 54 (February 22, 2007): A1–A8 (reporting on a paper by Matthew Woessner and Elizabeth Kelly-Woessner, "Left Pipeline: Why Conservatives Don't Get Doctorates").

reaching elite ranks. (One might wonder whether this factor, starting at a lower level of socioeconomic status, operates similarly for white and non-white academics, though.)

Another possible aspect of the issue has to do with the decline in adherence to the standard of scientific neutrality, or disinterestedness, in the American higher education system—the very standard that once made it possible to argue that a professor's political views were irrelevant to his or her research. Of the respondents in Gross and Simmons's survey, 70.9 percent said that it was all right for a professor's research to be guided by his or her political or religious beliefs; only 5.1 percent of liberal professors described themselves as "ardent advocates of neutrality." These data might be useful to anyone claiming that colleges and universities discriminate against people with conservative views. The data certainly don't *prove* discrimination, but they suggest the emergence of an ethos in which there is less aversion to weighing political views in evaluating merit than might have been the case thirty or forty years ago. If so, this would affect the career of someone whose views were outside the mainstream of the profession.

Still, the important lesson of the survey is not that the politics of the professoriate is liberal. The important lesson is that the politics of the professoriate is homogenous. Is this because of treatment effects? Are professors trained in a way that converts them to liberal opinions? Or is it a question of selection? Do people become professors because they are already liberal when they enter into their training? More significantly, is there a code, which would include opinions on political and social matters but would also include views on matters of intellectual, pedagogical, and collegial decorum, that entrants are required to demonstrate for admission to the profession? Does the profession select for attitudes about how the academic system works, about standards for performance, even about personal manner and appearance? The higher the barriers to entry in an occupation, the more likely there are to be implicit codes that need to be mastered in addition to the explicit entrance requirements. And the profession of college professor has a pretty high threshold. In fact, the height of the threshold may explain a lot of what we see in these studies of professors' politics.

3.

A national conversation about the condition and future of the PhD has been going on for about ten years. The conversation has been greatly helped by two major studies: "Re-envisioning the PhD," which was conducted by researchers at the University of Washington, and "PhDs—Ten Years Later," which was carried out at Berkeley.[16] Both studies identified roughly the same areas where the investigators thought that reform is desirable in doctoral education. These are: interdisciplinarity, practical training, and time to degree.

The studies were necessary in part because data on graduate education are notoriously difficult to come by. Until very recently, departments tended not to track their graduate students very assiduously. Departments knew how many students they admitted, and they knew how many they graduated; but they did not have a handle on what happened in

---

[16] "Re-envisioning the PhD," at http://www.grad.washington.edu/envision/, and "PhDs—Ten Years Later," University of California at Berkeley (1999). The latter study was run by Marisi Nerad.

between—that is, on where students were in their progress through the program. This was partly because of the pattern of benign neglect that is historically an aspect of the culture of graduate education in the United States, and it was partly because when some students finish in four years and other students in the same program finish in twelve years, there is really no meaningful way to quantify what is going on. "Are you still here?" is a thought that often pops into a professor's head when she sees a vaguely familiar face in the hall. "Yes, I am still here," is the usual answer, "and I'm working on that Incomplete for you." There was also, traditionally, very little hard information about where students went after they graduated. Graduate programs today are increasingly asked to provide reports on job placement—although, for understandable reasons, these reports tend to emit an unnatural glow. An employed graduate, wherever he or she happens to be working, is ipso facto a successfully placed graduate, and, at that moment, departmental attention relaxes. What happens to people after their initial placement is largely a matter of rumor and self-report.[17]

English was one of the fields surveyed in the two studies of the PhD. It is useful to look at, in part because it is a large field where employment practices have a significance that goes beyond courses for English majors. What the surveys

---

[17] This has changed since 2000. A number of groups have started tracking PhD completion rates, instituting programs that fit PhDs to non-academic careers, and exploring ways to shorten the time to degree. This is partly in response to job market conditions, but partly to concern about the increased use of ABDs (graduate students who have completed "all but the dissertation") and post-docs (PhDs who do not have tenure-track positions) as inexpensive teaching labor.

suggest is that if doctoral education in English were a cartoon character, then about thirty years ago, it zoomed straight off a cliff, went into a terrifying fall, grabbed a branch on the way down, and has been clinging to that branch ever since. Things went south very quickly, not gradually, and then they stabilized. Statistically, the state of the discipline has been fairly steady for about twenty-five years, and the result of this is a kind of normalization of what in any other context would seem to be a plainly inefficient and intolerable process. The profession has just gotten used to a serious imbalance between supply and demand.

Up to half of all doctoral students in English drop out before getting their degrees (something that appears to be the case in doctoral education generally), and only about half of the rest end up with the jobs they entered graduate school to get—that is, tenured professorships.[18] Over the three decades since the branch was grabbed, a kind of protective shell has grown up around this process, a culture of "realism," in which exogenous constraints are internalized, and the very conditions that make doctoral education problematic are turned into elements of that education. Students are told from the very start, almost from the minute they apply to graduate school, that they are effectively entering a lottery. This has to have an effect on professional self-conception.

---

[18] *PhD Completion and Attrition: Analysis of Baseline Demographic Data from the PhD Completion Project* (Council of Graduate Schools, 2008). The study surveyed students who entered graduate programs from 1992–93 to 1994–95. After ten years, 31.7 percent of PhD students in the humanities had dropped out, 49.3 percent had completed the degree, and the rest, 19 percent, were continuing. Ten-year attrition rates were highest in mathematics and the physical sciences (36.9 percent), lowest in the life sciences (26.2 percent). See http://www.phdcompletion.org/quantitative/book1_quant.asp.

The hinge whereby things swung into their present align-
ment, the ledge of the cliff, is located somewhere around
1970. That is when a shift in the nature of the PhD occurred.
The shift was the consequence of a bad synchronicity, one
of those historical pincer effects where one trend intersects
with its opposite, when an upward curve meets a downward
curve. One arm of the pincer has to do with the increased
professionalization of academic work, the conversion of the
professoriate into a group of people who were more likely to
identify with their disciplines than with their campuses. This
had two, contradictory effects on the PhD: it raised and low-
ered the value of the degree at the same time. The value was
raised because when institutions began prizing research above
teaching and service, the dissertation changed from a kind of
final term paper into the first draft of a scholarly monograph.
The dissertation became more difficult to write because more
hung on its success, and the increased pressure to produce an
ultimately publishable work increased, in turn, the time to
achieving a degree. That was a change from the faculty point
of view. It enhanced the selectivity of the profession.

The change from the institutional point of view, though,
had the opposite effect. In order to raise the prominence of
research in their institutional profile, schools began adding
doctoral programs. Between 1945 and 1975, the number
of American undergraduates increased 500 percent, but the
number of graduate students increased by nearly 900 percent.[19] On the one hand, a doctorate was harder to get; on the

---

[19] Roger L. Geiger, "The Ten Generations of American Higher Education," in
Philip G. Altbach, Robert O. Berdahl, and Patricia J. Gumport, eds., *Ameri-
can Higher Education in the Twenty-first Century: Social, Political, and Economic
Challenges* (Baltimore: Johns Hopkins University Press, 1999), p. 61.

other, it became less valuable because the market began to be flooded with PhDs.

This fact registered after 1970, when the rapid expansion of American higher education abruptly slowed to a crawl, depositing on generational shores a huge tenured faculty and too many doctoral programs churning out PhDs. The year 1970 is also the point from which we can trace the decline in the proportion of students majoring in liberal arts fields, and, within that decline, a proportionally larger decline in undergraduates majoring in the humanities. In 1970–71, English departments awarded 64,342 bachelor's degrees; that represented 7.6 percent of all bachelor's degrees, including those awarded in non-liberal arts fields, such as business.[20] The only liberal arts category that awarded more degrees than English was history and social science, a category that combines several disciplines. Thirty years later, in 2000–01, the number of bachelor's degrees awarded in all fields was 50 percent higher than in 1970–71, but the number of degrees in English was down both in absolute numbers—from 64,342 to 51,419— and as a percentage of all bachelor's degrees, from 7.6 percent to around 4 percent.

Fewer students major in English. This means that the demand for English literature specialists has declined. Even if a department requires, say, a course in eighteenth-century literature of its majors, the fact that there are fewer majors means that there is less demand for eighteenth-century specialists. But although the average number of credit hours

---

[20] Data on degrees in this paragraph and the next are taken from Bachelor's degrees conferred by degree-granting institutions, by discipline division: Selected years, 1970–71 through 2005–06, *Digest of Education Statistics*.

devoted to courses in English literature has gone down over the last twenty years, the number one subject, measured by the credit hours that students devote to it, has remained the same. That subject is English composition. Who teaches that? Not, mainly, English PhDs. Mainly, ABDs—graduate students who have completed all but their dissertations. There is a sense in which the system is now designed to produce ABDs.

The same trend can be observed in most of the liberal arts fields. In 1971, 24,801 students received bachelor's degrees in mathematics and statistics, about 3 percent of all bachelor's degrees. In 2001, there were 11,171 undergraduate degrees in those fields, less than 1 percent of the total number.[21] Again, it is not that students do not take math; it is that fewer students need specialized courses in mathematics, which are the courses that graduate students are trained to teach. There was a similar fall-off in bachelor's degrees awarded in the social sciences and history. There was upward movement in only two major liberal arts areas: psychology and the life sciences. American higher education has been expanding, but the liberal arts part of the system has been shrinking.

The Berkeley study, "PhDs—Ten Years Later," was based on lengthy questionnaires sent to just under 6,000 people, in six fields, who received PhDs between 1982 and 1985. One of those fields was English. People who received their PhDs in English between 1982 and 1985 had a median time to degree of ten years. A third of them took more than eleven years to finish, and the median age at the time of comple-

---

[21] This trend was also discussed in chapter one, in connection with the disjunction between liberal and pre-professional education.

tion was thirty-five. By 1995, 53 percent of those with PhDs that had been awarded from ten to fifteen years earlier had tenure; another 5 percent were in tenure-track positions. This means that about two fifths of English PhDs were effectively out of the profession as it is usually understood. (Some of these people were non-tenure-track faculty, and some were educational administrators. Most of the rest worked in what is called BGN—business, government, and NGOs.) Of those who had tenure, less than a fifth had positions in the kind of research universities in which they had been trained—that is, about 5 percent of all English PhDs. PhDs who began in a tenure-track position took an average of 6.1 years to get tenure. PhDs who began in non-tenure track positions but who eventually received tenure, which about half did, took an average of 8.1 years to get tenure.

The placement rate for PhDs has fluctuated. Between 1989 and 1996, the number of starting positions advertised in history dropped 11 percent; in art and art history, 26 percent; in foreign languages, 35 percent; and in political science, 37 percent. Yet every year during that period, universities gave out more PhDs than they had the year before.[22] It was plain that the supply curve had completely lost touch with the demand curve in American academic life. That meant if not quite a lost generation of scholars, a lost cohort. This was a period that coincided with attacks on the university for "political correctness," and it is not a coincidence that many of the most

---

[22] Figures are from my article "How to Make a PhD Matter," *New York Times Magazine*, September 22, 1996, p. 78. The rise and fall in the number of starting positions advertised annually is obviously to some degree a function of the economy; changes in tax revenues have an impact on hiring at public institutions on almost a yearly basis.

prominent critics of academia were themselves graduate school dropouts: Dinesh D'Souza, Roger Kimball, Richard Bernstein, David Lehman.[23] Apart from their specific criticisms and their politics, they articulated a widespread mood of disenchantment with the university as a congenial place to work.

There were efforts after 1996 to cut down the size of doctoral programs, with apparently some positive effect on the job market. But time-to-degree numbers did not improve. In the sixties, the time to degree as a registered student was about 4.5 years in the natural sciences and about six years in the humanities.[24] The current median time to degree in the humanities is nine years. That does not include what is called stop-time, which is when students take a leave or drop out for a semester or longer. And it obviously does not take into account students who never finish. It is not nine years from the receipt of the bachelor's degree, either; it is nine years as a registered student in a graduate program. The median total time it takes to achieve a degree in the humanities including stop-time is 11.3 years. In the social sciences, it is ten years, or 7.8 as a registered student. In the natural sciences, time to degree as a registered student is just under seven years.[25]

---

[23] Richard Bernstein, *Dictatorship of Virtue: Multiculturalism and the Battle for America's Future* (New York: Knopf, 1994); David Lehman, *Signs of the Times: Deconstruction and the Fall of Paul de Man* (New York: Poseidon, 1991). D'Souza was a graduate student at Princeton, Kimball at Yale, Bernstein at Harvard, and Lehman at Columbia.

[24] Christopher Jencks and David Riesman, *The Academic Revolution* (Garden City, NY: Doubleday, 1968), p. 536.

[25] Thomas B. Hoffer and Vincent Welch, Jr., "Time to Degree of U.S. Research Doctorate Recipients," *InfoBrief* (Washington, DC: National Science Foundation, March 2006), pp. 2–3.

If we put all these numbers together, we get the following composite: only about half of the people who enter doctoral programs in English finish them, and only about half of those who finish end up as tenured faculty, the majority of them at institutions that are not research universities. An estimate of the total elapsed time from college graduation to tenure would be somewhere between fifteen and twenty years. It is a lengthy apprenticeship.

That it takes longer to get a PhD in the humanities than it does in the social or natural sciences (although those fields also have longer times-to-degree than they once did) seems anomalous, since normally a dissertation in the humanities does not require extensive archival, field, or laboratory work. William Bowen and Neil Rudenstine, in their landmark study *In Pursuit of the PhD*, suggested that one reason for this might be that the paradigms for scholarship in the humanities have become less clear.[26] People are uncertain just what research in the humanities is supposed to constitute, and graduate students therefore spend an inordinate amount of time trying to come up with a novel theoretical twist on canonical texts or an unusual contextualization. Inquiry in the humanities has become quite eclectic without becoming contentious. This makes it a challenge for entering scholars to know where to make their mark.

[26] William G. Bowen and Neil L. Rudenstine, *In Pursuit of the PhD* (Princeton: Princeton University Press, 1992), p. 255. The authors analyze data on completion, attrition, and time-to-degree rates (pp. 105–41). They conclude that three eras "stand out": up to 1962, when time-to-degree rates rose; the 1960s, when they dropped back to earlier levels; and after the early seventies, when the time to degree "seems to have risen steadily and significantly in essentially all fields of study" (p. 116). Note, however, that their book was published in 1992.

The conclusion of the researchers who compiled the statistics on English PhDs for the Berkeley study was, See? It's not so bad! The reason they give for this is the reason that is often heard when the issues of time to degree and job placement are raised, which is that most people who get PhDs, whether they end up teaching or not, report high job satisfaction. (Job satisfaction is actually higher among PhDs with non-academic careers than it is among academics, partly because spousal problems—commuting marriages—are not as great outside academia.) And the majority say that they do not regret the time they spent in graduate school (although they have a lot of complaints about the quality of the mentorship they received). Students continue to check into the doctoral motel, and they don't seem terribly eager to check out. They like being in a university, and, since there is usually plenty of demand for their quite inexpensive teaching, universities like having them. Business is good. Where is the problem?[27]

The effort to reinvent the PhD as a degree qualifying people for non-academic as well as academic employment, to make the degree more practical, was an initiative of the Woodrow Wilson Foundation when it was headed by Robert Weisbuch.[28] These efforts are a worthy form of humanitarianism; but there is no obvious efficiency in requiring people to

[27] This was a common response to the report: that the vast majority of PhDs surveyed were happily employed somewhere, although a large number were doing work they were not specifically trained for, suggested that social investment in doctoral education was not wasted. See, among others, Peggy Maki and Nancy A. Borkowski, *The Assessment of Doctoral Education: Emerging Criteria and New Models for Improving Outcomes* (Sterling, VA: Stylus, 2006), pp. 109–41.

[28] Weisbuch was president of the foundation from 1997 to 2005; he left to become president of Drew University.

devote ten or more years to the mastery of a specialized area of scholarship on the theory that they are developing skills in research, or critical thinking, or communication. Professors are not themselves, for the most part, terribly practical people, and practical skills are not what they are trained to teach. They are trained to teach people to do what they do and to know what they know. Those skills and that knowledge are not self-evidently transferable. The ability to analyze *Finnegans Wake* does not translate into an ability to analyze a stock offering. If a person wanted to analyze stock offerings, he should not waste his time with Joyce. He should go to business school. Or get a job analyzing stock offerings.[29]

4.

It may be that the increased time to degree, combined with the weakening job market for liberal arts PhDs, is what is responsible for squeezing the profession into a single ideological box. It takes three years to become a lawyer. It takes four years to become a doctor. But it takes from six to nine years, and sometimes longer, to be eligible to teach poetry to college students for a living. Tightening up the oversight on student progress might reduce the time to degree by a little, but as long as the requirements remain, as long as students in most disciplines have general exams, field (or oral) exams, and monograph-length dissertations, it is not easy to see how the reduction will be significant. What is clear is that students who

---

[29] The remark is not offered glibly. I started in a professional school before going to a liberal arts graduate school; the discursive realms are very different. The non-transferability of specialized academic expertise is a jealously guarded feature of the profession, for reasons discussed in chapter three.

spend eight or nine years in graduate school are being seriously overtrained for the jobs that are available. The argument that they need the training to be qualified to teach undergraduates is belied by the fact that they are already teaching undergraduates. Undergraduate teaching is part of doctoral education; at many institutions, graduate students begin teaching classes the year they arrive. And the idea that the doctoral thesis is a rigorous requirement is belied by the quality of most doctoral theses. If every graduate student were required to publish a single peer-reviewed article instead of writing a thesis, the net result would probably be a plus for scholarship.

One pressure on universities to reduce radically the time to degree is simple humanitarianism. Lives are warped because of the length and uncertainty of the doctoral education process. Many people drop in and drop out and then drop in again; a large proportion of students never finish; and some people have to retool at relatively advanced ages. Put in less personal terms, there is a huge social inefficiency in taking people of high intelligence and devoting resources to training them in programs that half will never complete and for jobs that most will not get. Unfortunately, there is an institutional efficiency, which is that graduate students constitute a cheap labor force. There are not even search costs involved in appointing a graduate student to teach. The system works well from the institutional point of view not when it is producing PhDs, but when it is producing ABDs. It is mainly ABDs who run sections for lecture courses and they often offer courses of their own. The longer students remain in graduate school, the more people are available to staff undergraduate classes. Of course, overproduction of PhDs also creates a buyer's advantage in the market for academic labor. These circumstances explain the graduate student union movement that has been going on in higher education since the mid-1990s.[30]

But the main reason for academics to be concerned about the time it takes to get a degree has to do with the barrier this represents to admission to the profession. The obstacles to entering the academic profession are now so well known that the students who brave them are already self-sorted before they apply to graduate school. A college student who has some interest in further education, but who is unsure whether she wants a career as a professor, is not going to risk investing eight or more years finding out. The result is a narrowing of the intellectual range and diversity of those entering the field, and a widening of the philosophical and attitudinal gap that separates academic from non-academic intellectuals. Students who go to graduate school already talk the talk, and they learn to walk the walk as well. There is less ferment from the bottom than is healthy in a field of intellectual inquiry. Liberalism needs conservatism, and orthodoxy needs heterodoxy, if only in order to keep on its toes.

And the obstacles at the other end of the process, the anxieties over placement and tenure, do not encourage iconoclasm either. The academic profession in some areas is not reproducing itself so much as cloning itself. If it were easier and cheaper to get in and out of the doctoral motel, the disciplines would have a chance to get oxygenated by people who are much less invested in their paradigms. And the gap

---

[30] For responses and analysis, see Cary Nelson, ed., *Will Teach for Food: Academic Labor in Crisis* (Minneapolis: University of Minnesota Press, 1997), on the graduate student unionization movement, and Marc Bousquet, *How the University Works: Higher Education and the Low-Wage Nation* (New York: New York University Press, 2008), on the rise of "contingent faculty."

between inside and outside academia, which is partly created by the self-sorting, increases the hostility of the non-academic world toward what goes on in university departments, especially in the humanities. The hostility makes some disciplines less attractive to college students, and the cycle continues.

The moral of the story that the numbers tell once seemed straightforward: if there are fewer jobs for people with PhDs, then universities should stop giving so many PhDs—by making it harder to get into a PhD program (reducing the number of entrants) or harder to get through (reducing the number of graduates). But this has not worked. Possibly the story has a different moral, which is that there should be a lot *more* PhDs, and they should be much easier to get. The non-academic world would be enriched if more people in it had exposure to academic modes of thought, and had thereby acquired a little understanding of the issues that scare terms like "deconstruction" and "postmodernism" are attempts to deal with. And the academic world would be livelier if it conceived of its purpose as something larger and more various than professional reproduction—and also if it had to deal with students who were not so neurotically invested in the academic intellectual status quo. If PhD programs were determinate in length—if getting a PhD were like getting a law degree—then graduate education might acquire additional focus and efficiency. It might also attract more of the many students who, after completing college, yearn for deeper immersion in academic inquiry, but who cannot envision spending six years or more struggling through a graduate program and then finding themselves virtually disqualified for anything but a teaching career that they cannot count on having.

It is unlikely that the opinions of the professoriate will ever be a true reflection of the opinions of the public; and, in any case, that would be in itself an unworthy goal. Fostering a greater diversity of views within the professoriate *is* a worthy goal, however. The evidence suggests that American higher education is going in the opposite direction. Professors tend increasingly to think alike because the profession is increasingly self-selected. The university may not explicitly require conformity on more than scholarly matters, but the existing system implicitly demands and constructs it.

CONCLUSION

MY AIM has been to throw some light from history on a few problems in contemporary higher education. If there is a conclusion to be drawn from this exercise, it might be that the academic system is a deeply internalized one. The key to reform of almost any kind in higher education lies not in the way that knowledge is produced. It lies in the way that the producers of knowledge are produced. Despite transformational changes in the scale, missions, and constituencies of American higher education, professional reproduction remains almost exactly as it was a hundred years ago. Doctoral education is the horse that the university is riding to the mall. People are taught— more accurately, people are socialized, since the process selects for other attributes in addition to scholarly ability—to become expert in a field of specialized study; and then, at the end of a long, expensive, and highly single-minded process of credentialization, they are asked to perform tasks for which they have had no training whatsoever: to teach their fields to non-specialists, to connect what they teach to issues that students are likely to confront in the world outside the university, to be interdisciplinary, to write for a general audience, to justify their work to people outside their discipline and outside the academy. If we want professors to be better at these things, then we ought to train them differently.

Still, as is the case with every potential reform in academic life, there are perils. The world of knowledge production is a marketplace, but it is a very special marketplace, with its own practices, its own values, and its own rules. A lot has changed in higher education in the last fifty years. What has not changed is the delicate and somewhat paradoxical relation in which the university stands to the general culture. It is important for research and teaching to be relevant, for the university to engage with the public culture and to design its investigative paradigms with actual social and cultural life in view. That is, in fact, what most professors try to do—even when they feel inhibited from saying so by the taboo against instrumentalist and presentist talk. Professors teach what they teach because they believe that it makes a difference. To continue to do this, academic inquiry, at least in some fields, may need to become less exclusionary and more holistic. That may be the road down which the debates I have been describing are taking higher education.

But at the end of this road there is a danger, which is that the culture of the university will become just an echo of the public culture. That would be a catastrophe. It is the academic's job in a free society to serve the public culture by asking questions the public doesn't want to ask, investigating subjects it cannot or will not investigate, and accommodating voices it fails or refuses to accommodate. Academics need to look to the world to see what kind of teaching and research needs to be done, and how they might better train and organize themselves to do it. But they need to ignore the world's demand that they reproduce its self-image.

ACKNOWLEDGMENTS

THREE of the chapters in this book originated as the Page-Barbour Lectures at the University of Virginia, which I had the honor and pleasure of giving in February 2008. I am grateful to my excellent hosts in Virginia—Charles Mathewes, Tal Brewer, and Aaron Wall—and to the members of the university community who came to the talks, made challenging and useful interventions, and generally showed me a really good time. Chapter two was published, in a different form, as an occasional paper by the American Council of Learned Societies, through the kindness of the late John D'Arms; an earlier version appeared in *The New York Review of Books*. The Page-Barbour Lectures are by custom published by the University of Virginia Press. I thank the committee and the press for agreeing to let me have them published elsewhere. Elsewhere is W. W. Norton, and I am grateful to Roby Harrington and Robert Weil for their long-term interest in this project and for their editorial hands-on. And thanks to Skip Gates for making it all possible. I did some of the work on this book when I was a fellow at the Cullman Center for Writers and Scholars at the New York Public Library. The director of the center, Jean Strouse, and her staff provided an unusually collegial working environment.

I have been giving talks about and participating in conferences on higher education for many years, and a list of all the places where I have had a chance to share my ideas and to learn from colleagues in the academic world would be impractical. Academics love shoptalk at least as much as anyone else. I have visited dozens of schools and organizations, and I always found terrific people to talk to, but I do want to acknowledge several individuals who gave me special opportunities to speak, write, and learn about higher education and its problems: Jesse Ausubel, of the Alfred P. Sloan Foundation and the Richard Lounsbery Foundation; Peter Brooks, of the Whitney Humanities Center at Yale; William Kelly, of the Graduate Center of the City University of New York; Alvin Kernan, of the Andrew W. Mellon Foundation; Paul Kjellberg, of Whittier College; Gerald Marzorati, of *Harper's* and the *New York Times Magazine*; Robert Orrill, of the College Board; Linda Ray Pratt, of the American Association of University Professors; Robert Scholes, of the Modern Language Association; David Wiggins and Alan Ryan, of New College, Oxford; and a longtime and generous interlocutor on academic life, Jeffrey Williams, of Carnegie Mellon University.

I was fortunate when I came to Harvard to be invited to participate in a reform of the undergraduate curriculum undertaken at the direction of the president, Lawrence Summers, and the dean of the Faculty of Arts and Sciences, William Kirby. I learned a lot from them, and from many colleagues, during my involvement in that enterprise. I thank especially, for their friendship and our work together, Evelynn Hammonds, Andrew Knoll, Charles Maier, Steven Pinker,

Michael Sandel, Kay Shelemay, Diana Sorensen, and Maria Tatar. The road was longer and rockier than anyone probably anticipated, but reforms were accomplished. I was lucky to be in the game to the end, and to work with Derek Bok, Drew Faust, David Fithian, Dick Gross, and Jeremy Knowles. They taught me a great deal about how universities actually work, and much of what is in this book, not to mention the urge to write it, is informed by our collective experience. Above and beyond all else, I salute, in gratitude, the six intrepid souls to whom the book is dedicated: Stephanie Kenen, Stephen Kosslyn, David Liu, David Pilbeam, Alison Simmons, and Mary Waters.

INDEX

ABOUT THE AUTHOR

Louis Menand is Anne T. and Robert M. Bass Professor of English at Harvard. He has also taught at Princeton, Queens College, and the Graduate Center of the City University of New York, where he was Distinguished Professor of English. He is the author of several books, including *The Metaphysical Club*, which won the Pulitzer Prize for History in 2002. He has been associate editor at *The New Republic* (1986–87), literary editor at *The New Yorker* (1993–94), and contributing editor at *The New York Review of Books* (1994–2001). Since 2001, he has been a staff writer at *The New Yorker*.